编 委

郝文杰	全国民航职业教育教学指导委员会副秘书长、中国民航管理干部学院副教授
江丽容	全国民航职业教育教学指导委员会委员、国际金钥匙学院福州分院院长
林增学	桂林旅游学院旅游学院党委书记
丁永玲	武汉商学院旅游管理学院教授
史金鑫	中国民航大学乘务学院民航空保系主任
刘元超	西南航空职业技术学院空保学院院长
杨文立	上海民航职业技术学院安全员培训中心主任
范月圆	江苏航空职业技术学院航空飞行学院副院长
定 琦	郑州旅游职业学院现代服务学院副院长
黄 华	浙江育英职业技术学院航空学院副院长
王姣蓉	武汉商贸职业学院现代管理技术学院院长
毛颖善	珠海城市职业技术学院旅游管理学院副院长
黄华勇	毕节职业技术学院航空学院副院长
魏 日	江苏旅游职业学院旅游学院副院长
吴 云	上海旅游高等专科学校外语学院院长
穆广宇	三亚航空旅游职业学院民航空保系主任
田 文	中国民航大学乘务学院民航空保系讲师
汤 黎	武汉职业技术学院旅游与航空服务学院副教授
江 群	武汉职业技术学院旅游与航空服务学院副教授
汪迎春	浙江育英职业技术学院航空学院副教授
段莎琪	张家界航空工业职业技术学院副教授
王勤勤	江苏航空职业技术学院航空飞行学院副教授
覃玲媛	广西蓝天航空职业学院航空管理系主任
付 翠	河北工业职业技术大学空乘系主任
李 岳	青岛黄海学院空乘系主任
王观军	福州职业技术学院空乘系主任
王海燕	新疆职业大学空中乘务系主任
谷建云	湖南女子学院管理学院副教授
牛晓斐	湖南女子学院管理学院讲师

高等职业学校"十四五"规划民航服务类系列教材

民航客舱服务播音技巧

主　编 ◎ 徐菲菲
副主编 ◎ 杨红艳　左红伟

华中科技大学出版社
http://press.hust.edu.cn
中国·武汉

图书在版编目(CIP)数据

民航客舱服务播音技巧/徐菲菲主编. —武汉:华中科技大学出版社,2021.8(2025.1重印)
ISBN 978-7-5680-7300-4

Ⅰ.①民… Ⅱ.①徐… Ⅲ.①民用航空-乘务人员-商业服务-播音-语言艺术-高等职业教育-教材
Ⅳ.①F560.9

中国版本图书馆 CIP 数据核字(2021)第 165021 号

民航客舱服务播音技巧 徐菲菲 主编
Minhang Kecang Fuwu Boyin Jiqiao

策划编辑:胡弘扬
责任编辑:陈　然
封面设计:廖亚萍
责任校对:李　琴
责任监印:周治超

出版发行:华中科技大学出版社(中国·武汉)　　电话:(027)81321913
　　　　　武汉市东湖新技术开发区华工科技园　　邮编:430223
录　　排:华中科技大学惠友文印中心
印　　刷:武汉开心印印刷有限公司
开　　本:787mm×1092mm　1/16
印　　张:10
字　　数:280 千字
版　　次:2025 年 1 月第 1 版第 5 次印刷
定　　价:42.80 元

本书若有印装质量问题,请向出版社营销中心调换
全国免费服务热线:400-6679-118　竭诚为您服务
版权所有　侵权必究

PREFACE
前言

2023年是贯彻落实党的二十大精神、以中国式现代化全面推进中华民族伟大复兴开局之年,是全面建设社会主义现代化国家开局起步的关键时期。加快构建民航客舱服务新发展格局,构建优质高效的民航客舱服务播音技巧新机制,是着力推动民航客舱服务高质量发展必由之路。随着航空事业的发展和旅客需求的不断提高,旅客对空中服务质量的要求也越来越高。现代化的客舱服务不仅要求空中乘务员熟练掌握服务的程序和规范,更重要的是要求空中乘务员有强烈的服务意识。客舱的服务质量,对于旅客对航空公司的满意度起着决定性的作用,是航空公司核心竞争力的关键。客舱服务的核心内容和重点工作就是为广大旅客出行提供方便快捷的空中服务,因此必须不断提高航空公司客舱整体服务质量和水平,以期对航空事业的健康良性发展起到积极的推动作用。

空中乘务客舱广播作为空中服务的重要内容,在航空公司发展进程中扮演着重要角色,它架起飞机客舱内沟通的桥梁,是客舱文化的重要组成部分。空中乘务员语言水平的高低,直接体现了一个航空公司服务质量的好坏,其作为航空公司的形象代言人,始终代表着航空公司的整体运营理念。空中乘务员语言交际能力的提高显然是保障高质量服务的重要条件,需要空中乘务员能够使用文明用语、规范发音,做好航空信息的传递工作,用真心去服务,用真诚换取旅客的理解,用微笑获得旅客的支持。要提高空中乘务员的播音质量,通过高水平的播报和良好的客舱服务,将航班信息更好地传达给旅客,给旅客带去舒适的旅途体验,进而提升空中服务质量。同时,空中乘务员要提高个人的语言修养,保证沟通的流畅,致力于提升航空服务的整体水平。

本书深入浅出系统地阐述了民航客舱服务播音技巧的基础知识、基本理论,提出了民航客舱广播播音用语的规范和要求,并融入广播播音用词的政治素养和道德情操,通过专业课程与课程思政的有机融合,深入挖掘课程思政因素,提炼专业课程中的传统文化美德、人文主义精神等优秀文化传统和价值取向,以提高民航客舱服务的职业素养和综合素质。本书分为七个模块,具体内容包括机上服务广播概述、机上服务广播常用词汇和表达、起飞前服务广播、飞行中服务广播、着陆后服务广播、飞行中特殊情况服务广播、介绍性广播。每个模块通过项目目标的设定,启发学生对各单元内容的思考,通过项目任务的引入和列举的大量具体实例,更加直观地帮助专业教师进行课堂授课和学生具体实践。书中讲到,客舱服务播音技巧是空中乘务员借助一定的语言和语调,在服务过程中,表达清晰,语态准确,语速均匀,语调恰当,使旅客有愉快和亲切之感,又能准确清晰地传达广播信息,使旅客对空乘服务工作产生良好的印象。认真掌握服务语言是提高客舱服务质量的关键。提高空中乘务员的语言水平,增强个人语言魅力,有利于空中乘务员树立良好的职业形象。

本书由江苏航空职业技术学院徐菲菲担任主编,江苏航空职业技术学院左红伟和杨红艳担任副主编,江苏航空职业技术学院乔杉负责录制音频,全书由徐菲菲统稿整理。本书的初稿曾作为江苏航空职业技术学院空乘系学生教学使用,几经修改得以完善。江苏航空职业技术学院航空飞行学院对本书编写给予了大力的支持与帮助。编写过程中参考了一些书籍及相关网站的内容,在此一并致以诚挚的感谢。

由于编者能力有限,加之编写时间仓促,书中难免存在不足与疏漏之处,恳请各位专家和读者批评、指正。

编　者

为便于读者有效进行播音训练,本书提供了广播词音频教学资源,便于读者练习。

读者第一次登录,需要利用智能手机通过微信扫描二维码,授权进入注册页面,填写注册信息。按照提示输入手机号,获取验证码,并设置登录密码,点击立即注册,注册成功。

读者通过手机第一次登录成功,以后可直接在微信端扫码登录,重复查看教学资源。

CONTENTS 目录

项目一 | **机上服务广播概述** ………………………………………………… 1
  任务一 客舱服务概述 ……………………………………………………… 2
  任务二 播音员基本素质 …………………………………………………… 11
  任务三 客舱播音技巧训练 ………………………………………………… 14

项目二 | **机上服务广播常用词汇和表达** ……………………………… 22
  任务一 机场广播常用词汇和表达 ………………………………………… 22
  任务二 客舱服务广播常用词汇和表达 …………………………………… 23
  任务三 客舱安全广播常用词汇和表达 …………………………………… 26
  任务四 机场主要设施词汇 ………………………………………………… 29

项目三 | **起飞前服务广播** ………………………………………………… 32
  任务一 登机广播 …………………………………………………………… 32
  任务二 欢迎乘机 …………………………………………………………… 38
  任务三 安全演示 …………………………………………………………… 41
  任务四 安全检查 …………………………………………………………… 45
  任务五 起飞前再次确认安全检查 ………………………………………… 49
  任务六 行李托运 …………………………………………………………… 51

项目四 | **飞行中服务广播** ………………………………………………… 56
  任务一 起飞后安全广播 …………………………………………………… 56
  任务二 平飞后休息提醒 …………………………………………………… 61

项目五 | **着陆后服务广播** ………………………………………………… 66
  任务一 着陆广播 …………………………………………………………… 66
  任务二 滑行广播 …………………………………………………………… 70

		任务三 下机广播	73
		任务四 转机广播	75

项目六 | 飞行中特殊情况服务广播 …… 80

  任务一 飞机延误 …… 80
  任务二 疫情防控 …… 87
  任务三 颠簸广播 …… 90
  任务四 寻求医护帮助广播 …… 98
  任务五 客舱释压指导 …… 102
  任务六 失火状况广播 …… 104
  任务七 灭火后广播 …… 109

项目七 | 介绍性广播 …… 112

  任务一 航空公司介绍 …… 112
  任务二 节日介绍 …… 121
  任务三 欢迎词介绍 …… 123
  任务四 风景介绍 …… 126
  任务五 城市介绍 …… 134

项目一　机上服务广播概述

项目目标

- **知识目标**
  掌握民航客舱广播播音用语的规范和要求；
  了解民航客舱广播员的基本素质和要求。
- **能力目标**
  能规范使用客舱广播播音用语。
- **素质目标**
  感悟空中乘务人员的职业精神，提高空中乘务人员的综合职业素养。

知识框架

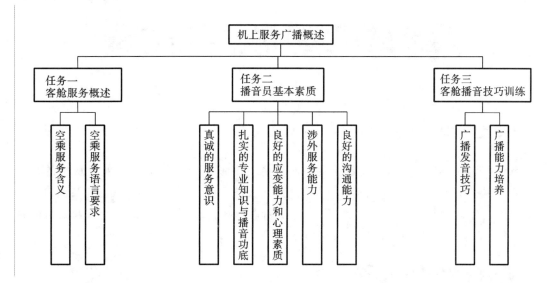

项目引入

厦航一直以来致力于培养和选拔优秀的客舱广播员。为了让更多的旅客通过声音感受到厦航传递的真诚与温暖，让更多优秀的乘务员施展才华，厦航组织了首次客舱高级广播员选拔大赛。考核设立了以下四个环节。

环节一：自我介绍

全国各地的考生各显神通,有通过诗句引出名字的,有用英文演绎美剧中经典桥段的,还有通过中、英、法三国语言展示强大外语水平的。

环节二：即兴广播

考生们准确的翻译、流畅的表达、扎实的业务、敏捷的思维让评委们感受到了他们强大的实力。

环节三：新闻播报

评委老师说,这个环节是最考验广播员播音功底的环节。

环节四：给词说事

这是难度较大的一个环节,选手需要根据给出的三个关键词进行论述。考生们顶住压力,思绪迸发,联想到生活,联系到厦航,上升到国家,展现了他们超强的应变能力和语言组织能力。

(资料来源:https://baijiahao.baidu.com/s? id=1640747349859278880.)

阅读后思考

1. 你认为客舱广播在机上服务工作中的重要性如何？为什么？
2. 你所了解的空乘播音技巧有哪些？标准的客舱广播是怎样的？
3. 优秀的客舱广播员应具备哪些基本素质？分析自己存在的差距。

任务一　客舱服务概述

一、空乘服务含义

空乘,即空中乘务人员,是飞机上为旅客服务的专职工作人员。空乘人员从事的是一种特殊的服务工作,由于其在高空作业,相比其他服务行业,该职业带有一种高端色彩。这个职业的工作内容具有规范性强、工作环境封闭性高的特点,促成了该行业从业人员的高收入,吸引了很多人进入空乘行业。

（一）客舱服务内容

客舱服务包括礼仪、沟通、卫生、广播、救助、餐饮、娱乐、咨询服务等方面。在客舱服务过程中,乘务员应使用礼貌用语,热情迎送旅客,主动帮助旅客安排座位及安放随身携带的物品。起飞前应介绍紧急设备的使用方法及注意事项,机长应向旅客做自我介绍。航行中要介绍航线主要地标、名胜古迹及地理情况。一般来说,飞行时间超过2小时且正值供餐时间或飞行时间超过3小时,会供应正餐;飞行时间超过1.5小时且非供餐时间或飞行时间超过2小时,会供应点心。此外,客舱服务还包括提供杂志和当天或前一天的中外文报纸(人手一份)、机上录像(内容要轻松、活泼、健康并每月更换一次)及清洁卫生等事项。现代交通运输业的激烈竞争对客舱服务的规范化、个性化、高端化提出了更高的要求。

(二)客舱服务阶段

客舱服务一般包含三个阶段。

1 上机前准备阶段

上机前准备阶段是指从客舱乘务员接受航班任务到上飞机之前的阶段,它是执行空乘工作的起始阶段,基本在上机前完成,是保证服务质量的重要环节。

乘务员在接受航班任务后,应及时到公司网站了解航班情况,包括航线、航班号、机型、起降时间、航班性质、签到时间、机组乘车时间、乘务组成员信息等,做好准备工作,按时签到,参加航前准备会。在准备会上要明确航班各方面的信息。乘务员在执行任务时必须携带登机证、乘务员执照、健康证等证件,以及乘务员手册、广播词及其他服务用品。这个阶段要求乘务员熟练操作飞机上的各种设备,熟知遇到紧急情况时各个号位的乘务员的任务,整个机组还需协商好各种突发事件的应对措施。

2 机上准备阶段

在旅客登机前,乘务员需要按照分工号位的岗位职责要求提前1小时10分钟到岗,对机上的所有应急设备和服务设备进行检查。

首先要检查各种设备是否完好,如旅客服务面板上的阅读灯、呼唤铃、小桌板、桌椅靠背,乘务员服务面板上的各种灯光、话筒、音乐等,尤其要检查紧急状态下要用到的各种设备的情况,如氧气瓶里的氧气、灭火瓶、充气滑梯等。对广播设备、撤离设备、电器等要进行严格测试。确认厨房用具充足,清点餐食。检查厨房用品是否齐全,如茶叶、咖啡、方糖是否齐全,是否有特殊旅客餐等。检查客舱厕所卫生及用品情况,如面巾纸、卷纸、肥皂、香水、坐垫纸是否配备齐全。确认书报、杂志已整齐摆放在指定位置。确认毛毯、枕头等物品已按规定摆放整齐。按有关规定喷洒杀虫剂、清新剂等。随后,进行清舱工作,确保飞机上除机组人员外,无外来人员、外来物品。各项准备工作就绪后,乘务员需将准备情况报告乘务长。

3 空中服务实施阶段

空中服务实施阶段是指从旅客开始登机到飞机落地、乘务组下机的阶段,即与旅客直接互动的阶段,包含接待旅客、客舱安全检查和示范、发放供应品、巡视客舱等。这是客舱乘务员为旅客提供服务的主要阶段,能直接展现空乘人员的专业水平和航空公司的服务质量。

迎接旅客时,乘务员要文明礼貌、微笑服务,主动协助旅客安放行李,帮助老、幼、病、残、孕旅客尽快找到他们的座位。旅客登机后,乘务员要整理好行李架上的行李,确保安全、整洁。

旅客坐好、安放好行李后,外场乘务员就要进行客舱安全示范,随后进行客舱安全检查,包括调直椅背、收起小桌板、拉开遮阳板、系好安全带、扣好行李架、检查紧急出口和通道有无阻碍物等,提醒旅客手机关机或开启飞行模式。内场的乘务员还要把厨房电源关掉,扣好各种锁扣,放好餐车,关好卫生间的门。

飞机平稳飞行后,内场乘务员进行广播,外场乘务员就要开始发放报纸、纸巾等。为旅客发放供应品及食品时,应主动介绍物品名称。对特殊旅客提出的要求应尽量满足,不能做到时,应耐心解释。

飞行中,乘务员要随时巡视客舱状况。观察旅客动态,时时提醒旅客系好安全带,以防颠簸。保持客舱内的清洁和卫生,及时处理旅客需要帮助解决的问题。乘务员工作时脚步要轻,步伐要稳,以免影响旅客休息或给旅客带来一种烦躁紧张感。

■ **案例**

山东航空股份有限公司对乘务员迎客的规定

(1)旅客登机时,乘务长播放登机音乐,打开客舱灯光至高亮度,站在机舱门口迎客并负责与地面工作人员的交接和联系。

(2)客舱乘务员应站在合适位置迎客。

(3)乘务员应着装整齐、站姿端正、面带微笑、热情礼貌地迎接并问候旅客。

(4)重要旅客及其行李由指定客舱乘务员负责安放,并根据地面人员提供的VIP旅客名单,使用尊称或姓氏问好。

(5)有秩序地引导旅客入座,协助旅客放好随身携带物品。安排座位时,如果旅客有不方便的情况,起飞后,可与相邻旅客商量,做适当调整。

(6)对旅客要求托管的物品应妥善存放。为旅客保管衣物时,应确认其口袋内无贵重物品,如钱包、首饰、护照等。

(7)原则上不应为旅客保管药品、贵重物品或易碎物品。若必须为旅客保管,应向旅客说明责任,得到旅客同意后,方可接受。

(资料来源:《山东航空股份有限公司客舱乘务员手册》)。

二、空乘服务语言要求

对于以语言表达为主要服务内容的空乘人员来说,服务用语是事关服务质量和服务态度的重中之重。说话是人最基本的技能,也是人类主要的沟通方式。对空乘行业而言,在机场服务、机上服务中,语言服务几乎占到90%。从检票台换登机牌到安检口过安检,从候机口服务再到客舱内的安全示范、送餐、沟通、播音等,空乘人员都要用服务用语。旅客登机时的"欢迎乘机"、送餐时的"请问您需要吃点(喝点)什么"、安全检查时的"请收起小桌板"等常规服务,以及面对飞机不能按时降落时旅客的质问,都需要空乘人员与旅客进行语言沟通。认真掌握服务用语是提高服务质量的关键。空乘人员提高自己的语言水平,增强个人的语言魅力,有助于树立良好的职业形象。

空乘服务语言要求可以概括为以下几点。

（一）普通话要标准流利

空乘服务行业作为一个高端的服务行业，对空乘人员整体素质的要求越来越高，在航空服务高标准的要求下，能说一口标准的普通话，是合格的空乘人员必须具备的基本素质。一方面，一口标准的普通话与空乘人员的靓丽形象相得益彰；另一方面，有利于空乘人员与旅客交流。

对空乘人员来说，恰当的语言和成熟的沟通技巧是必不可少的，它们贯穿于机舱服务的各个方面。空乘人员接待旅客，与旅客交流，并在飞行过程中提供安全介绍、餐饮服务和其他服务都需要良好的沟通能力。提高空乘人员的沟通能力和普通话水平，不仅有利于空乘人员的工作发展，而且对提高航空公司的服务水平及质量、提高航空公司的整体形象起着重要作用。一般来说，空乘人员的普通话水平至少要达到二级乙等。

（二）语言服务要真诚亲切①

空乘语言是空乘人员借助一定的语言、语调，代表自己或航空公司与旅客进行交流的一种比较规范、比较灵活的口头用语。旅客服务满意度调查显示，服务语言是旅客评价服务质量的重要指标之一。在服务过程中，空乘人员的语言适当得体、清晰、悦耳，就会使旅客产生愉快、亲切之感，对其服务工作产生良好的印象；反之，如果空乘人员的服务语言生硬、唐突、刺耳，则会让旅客难以接受，有可能引起旅客的不满与投诉，给航空公司的形象带来严重的负面影响。

1. 语言服务贵在真诚

有诗云："功成理定何神速，速在推心置人腹。"说话的魅力，不在于说得多么流畅，多么滔滔不绝，而在于是否表达出真诚。真诚的语言，不论对说话者还是对听者，都至关重要。

当我们被某篇文章或某个电影情节打动的时候，多半是因为里面的话语真诚，而在与旅客沟通时，空乘人员的语言也同样需要真诚。只有态度诚恳，才能让人信服，才能达到让旅客满意的效果。当然，这种真诚并不是一点技巧也不讲，而是要掌握一点语言技巧，再结合恰到好处的表达方式。

2. 语言服务误区

轻易允诺旅客。在与旅客交流时，谈天说地可以轻松愉快，但是在服务旅客的过程中，交流到有关航空公司服务内容的时候，就一定要慎之又慎。一旦做出某些承诺，旅客就会认为你说的事情一定能办到，如果你做不到，那么你就是不守信用，很有可能遭到旅客投诉，并给航空公司带来不好的影响。

---

① 凌燕的博客《浅谈空中乘务员服务语言技巧》，http://blog.sina.com.cn/ceass。

轻易拒绝旅客。乘务员在服务旅客的过程中，经常会遇到旅客提出各种要求或条件，有些是乘务员能做到的，有些超出乘务员的能力范围，为了给旅客和自己留有余地，一般不要一口回绝。这样既能显示对对方的重视，也能为自己争取主动。乘务员可以想办法尽量满足旅客的要求，或者告诉旅客，我们虽然不能满足他们的要求，但可以用其他方式代替，然后征询旅客的意见，看这样的解决方法能否被接受。即使你不能为旅客解决问题，他们也会因为你的真诚，因为你以旅客为出发点的态度，而对你的服务给予充分的肯定。

话说绝对。话不能说得过于绝对，这是服务用语的基本要点，目的是要给自己留有余地。如果当场表态：这个绝对不行，那个绝对不可。再想回旋就没余地了，这样又会使自己陷入被动的局面，所以不要轻易判断孰是孰非，避免用"绝对""一定"等词语。

（三）服务语言要巧妙

服务语言的巧妙体现在多个方面。

1 认识旅客的需求

旅客的年龄、身份、心情、所在的环境不同，同样的一句话乘务员应该根据这些因素的不同，采取不同的表达方式。比如对年长者说话的时候乘务员要注意声音洪亮、语气缓和，尽量避免使用专业术语，最重要的就是要有耐心，试着站在对方的角度去考虑。年长者多是第一次坐飞机，而乘务员是每天都接触，自然对客舱环境熟悉，所以不要奇怪他们会提出这样或那样的问题，也不要奇怪你说多少遍，他们也不明白，总是问同样一件事。和年长者说话一定要注意话语简单直接，例如，乘务员问一位老奶奶需要喝什么饮料："阿姨，您想喝点什么饮料吗？"老奶奶回答："啊，是啊，我要喝饮料。"乘务员以为自己没说清楚，把声音提高、语速放慢再次询问了一遍，老奶奶也很认真地再次回答了一遍。如此反复，最终弄得谁也不开心，老奶奶认为乘务员不给她提供饮料，而乘务员委屈地认为是老奶奶没有提出明确的要求。其实这个很简单的案例就说明了我们没有站在旅客的角度去思考问题。老奶奶是想喝饮料的，可是她不知道该如何表达，乘务员如果意识到这一点，就应该把饮料瓶拿给她看并说："好的，这是苹果汁，这是橙汁，您喜欢喝哪一种呢？"老年人看到了直观的东西，自然就会明白并做出选择。所以乘务员的服务工作并不是简单的端茶倒水，即使是简单的动作，也要注意使用语言技巧。

2 巧妙地回应对方的意见

不论旅客对客舱服务接受还是拒绝，乘务员都要及时回应，而且要让旅客感受到乘务员的通情达理。例如，在供餐期间，当供应到某位旅客时，他所要的餐食品种刚好没有了，这时乘务员去找了一份头等舱的餐食拿给旅客，说："刚好头等舱多了一份餐，我就给您送来了"。旅客一听，很不高兴："什么意思，头等舱吃不了的给我吃？我不吃。"乘务员的好心反而换来旅客的不理解，究其原因，还是乘务员没有掌握说话的技巧，即使是要别人接受，也要让对方高兴地接受。如果换个方式说："真对不起，您要的餐食刚好没有了，您看我将头等舱的餐食给您可以吗？希望您能喜欢，在下一段航程中，我会优先请您选择餐食品种，我将非常愿意为您服务。"如何让对方乐意接受，这就体现在说话的艺术上。

3 通过语言化解双方的矛盾

当旅客间发生冲突时,一定要注意乘务员的目的是平息"风波",而不是解决矛盾。一般情况下,不要随便评论双方,即使是某一方讲了一些偏激之词,也不要刻意帮助另一方,不要带入"义愤""拔刀相助"等个人情绪,多用劝导式的语言;最合适的方法就是只劝停,不评论,进行模糊处理。可以使用婉转的语言缓解双方的负面情绪,减轻周围环境的紧张感,让双方平静下来,转化矛盾,从而大事化小,小事化了。

(四)能运用外语流利沟通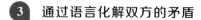

空乘人员的服务对象是来自世界各地说各种语言的旅客,空乘人员英语水平的高低,能体现一个航空公司服务质量的好坏。空乘人员语言交际能力的提高是保障高质量服务的重要条件。空乘人员要会使用简单的英语等与旅客进行交流。

下面是一些常用的航空服务英语单句。

1 登机

(1) 飞机起飞前30分钟,即上午9:30开始登机。
Boarding will start thirty minutes before departure at 9:30 a.m..
(2) 飞往悉尼的123次航班正在五号登机口登机。
Flight 123 to Sydney is now boarding at Gate 5.
(3) 乘坐飞往悉尼的123次航班的旅客现在请登机。
We are now boarding all passengers on flight 123 to Sydney.
(4) 我们很快要请部分旅客提前登机。
We'll begin pre-boarding soon.
(5) 头等舱和公务舱的旅客,以及带小孩或者需要特殊帮助的旅客现在请您开始登机。
At this time, we'd like to pre-board passengers in first class and business class, and passengers with young children or those who need special assistance.
(6) 现在请座位在13至29排之间的旅客登机。
We are now boarding passengers from row 13 to row 29.
(7) 现在请所有旅客登机。
Now we'd like to begin general boarding.

2 起飞前

(1) 由于天气恶劣,航班延误。
The flight has been delayed because of the bad weather.
(2) 由于能见度低,机场关闭,我们不能起飞。
We can't take off because the airport is closed due to poor visibility.
(3) 成都的天气不太好,所以飞机延误了。
The weather in Chengdu is not so good, so the flight has been delayed.

（4）早上好，女士（先生），欢迎登机！

Morning, madam(sir), welcome aboard!

（5）请允许我自我介绍，我是本次航班的乘务长。

May I introduce myself? I'm the chief purser of this flight.

（6）请跟我来，您的座位在客舱中部。

Follow me, please. Your seat is in the middle of the cabin.

（7）请稍等一下，我查查看。

Excuse me for a second, I'll check.

（8）飞机马上就要起飞了，请不要在客舱内走动。

The plane is about to take off. Please don't walk about in the cabin.

（9）中国国际航空公司CA687次航班，上午8:20起飞。

Air China Flight CA687 leaves at 8:20 in the morning.

3 飞行中

（1）您想喝点什么吗？

Would you like to drink anything?

（2）您想看报纸或杂志吗？

Would you like to read newspapers or magazines?

（3）我们的飞机目前比较颠簸，请系好安全带。

Our plane is bumping hard. Please keep your seat belt fastened.

4 紧急情况

（1）请马上系好安全带。由于飞机发动机发生故障，我们将紧急迫降。

Fasten your seat belt immediately. The plane will make an emergency landing because of the sudden breakdown of an engine.

（2）从座椅下拿出救生衣穿上！

Take out the life vest under your seat and put it on!

（3）戴上氧气面罩。

Put the mask over your face.

（4）把头弯下来，放在两膝之间！

Bend your head between your knees!

（5）弯下身，抓住脚。

Bend down and grab your ankle.

5 广播词

（1）欢迎词。

女士们、先生们：

早上/下午/晚上好！

欢迎您乘坐_____航班，您的座位号码在行李架下方。请将您所有的手提行李存放在行李架上或您前面的座椅下方。

找到座位的旅客请您尽快入座,以方便后面的旅客登机。

谢谢您的配合。

Good morning/afternoon/evening, ladies and gentlemen,

We are honored to welcome you aboard _____. Your seat number is indicated on the edge of the overhead compartment. Please kindly stow all your carry-on luggage securely in the overhead compartment or under the seat in front of you.

Please take your assigned seats as quickly as possible and leave the aisle clear for others to be seated.

We appreciate your cooperation. Thank you.

(2) 起飞广播。

女士们、先生们:

我们的飞机已经在跑道上滑行,准备起飞,请您系好安全带,调直座椅靠背,放下座椅扶手,收起小桌板、脚踏板,打开遮光板,并确认手机处于关闭状态。

现在由乘务员进行客舱安全检查。谢谢!

Ladies and gentlemen,

As our aircraft is taxiing into the runway for take-off, please put your seat back upright, secure your tray-table (and footrest) and put your armrests down. Please make sure that your seat belt is securely fastened, and your window shades are drawn up. All mobile phones must remain switched off at all times.

Flight attendants start safety check now. Thank you.

(3) 起飞后广播。

女士们、先生们:

我们的航班预计在北京时间/当地时间_____时_____分到达_____机场。飞机已经开始下降。现在,请您确认已系好安全带,收起小桌板,调直椅背,打开遮光板,取下耳机以及连接在座椅电源上的数据连接线,大型便携式电子设备已妥善存放。机上洗手间将暂停使用。谢谢!

Ladies and gentlemen,

Our flight will be landing at _____ Airport at _____ (Beijing time/Local time). We will start to descend in a few minutes. Please fasten your seat belt, pull up the window shade, put your tray table in place, bring your seat back upright, and unplug your headphones and electronic devices. Please make sure the large portable electronic devices are stowed properly. The lavatories will be closed. Thank you.

(4) 湍流广播。

各位旅客请注意,我们正遇到湍流,请您回到座位上并系好安全带。洗手间暂停使用,正在使用洗手间的旅客,请您注意抓好扶手。经历湍流期间,我们将暂停客舱服务,感谢您的理解。

Ladies and gentlemen,

We are now encountering some turbulence. Please return to your seat and fasten your seat belt. Lavatory is not to be used. When you are using lavatory, please hold the handle tightly. During turbulence, we will stop the cabin service. Thank you!

(5) 餐前广播。

女士们、先生们：

我们将为您提供餐食(点心餐)、茶水、咖啡和饮料,欢迎您选用。需要用餐的旅客,请您将小桌板放下。

为了方便其他旅客,在供餐期间,请您将座椅靠背调整到正常位置。谢谢！

Ladies and gentlemen,

We will be serving you meal(dessert) with tea, coffee and other soft drinks. Welcome to make your choice. Please put down the tray table in front of you.

For the convenience of the passenger behind you, please return your seat back to the upright position during the meal service. Thank you!

(6) 预计到达时间广播。

女士们、先生们：

本架飞机预计在_____分钟后到达_____。地面温度是_____,谢谢！

Ladies and gentlemen,

We will be landing at _____ Airport in about _____ minutes. The ground temperature is _____ degrees Celsius. Thank you!

(7) 下降时安全检查广播。

女士们、先生们：

飞机正在下降。请您回原位坐好,系好安全带,收起小桌板,将座椅靠背调整到正常位置。所有个人电脑及电子设备必须处于关闭状态。请您确认您的手提物品是否妥善安放。稍后,我们将调暗客舱灯光。

谢谢！

Ladies and gentlemen,

Our plane is descending now. Please be seated and fasten your seat belt. Seat backs and tables should be returned to the upright position. All personal computers and electronic devices should be turned off. And please make sure that your carry-on items are securely stowed. We will be dimming the cabin lights for landing.

Thank you!

(8) 到达终点站广播。

女士们、先生们：

飞机已经降落在_____机场。当地时间是_____,室外温度_____摄氏度(_____华氏度)。飞机正在滑行,为了您的安全,请您不要离开座位,等飞机完全停稳,安全带指示灯熄灭后,再解开安全带,整理好手提物品准备下飞机。从行李架取物品时,请注意安全。您交运的行李请到行李提取处领取。需要在本站转乘飞机到其他地方的旅客请到候机室中转柜办理手续。

欢迎您来到_____（城市）。感谢您选择_____航空公司，我们期待下次为您服务！祝您旅途愉快！

Ladies and gentlemen,

Our plane has landed at _____ Airport. The local time is _____. The temperature outside is _____ degrees Celsius(_____ degrees Fahrenheit). The plane is taxiing. For your safety, please stay in your seat for the time being. When the aircraft stops completely and the Fasten Seat Belt sign is turned off, please detach the seat belt, take all your carry-on items and disembark. Please be careful when retrieving items from the overhead compartment. Your checked baggage may be claimed in the baggage claim area. The transit passengers please go to the connection flight counter in the waiting hall to complete the procedures.

Welcome to _____(city). Thank you for selecting _____ Airline for your travel today and we look forward to serving you again. Wish you a pleasant day!

（9）旅客下飞机广播。

女士们、先生们：

本架飞机已经完全停稳，请您从前/中/后登机门下飞机。谢谢！

Ladies and gentlemen,

The plane has stopped completely, please disembark from the front/middle/rear entry door. Thank you!

任务二　播音员基本素质

在当前航空公司竞争激烈的环境下，客舱服务质量已经成为旅客选择航空公司的新标准。空中乘务员的第一职责就是为旅客服务，客舱播音服务作为传播信息的重要工具，播音员的服务意识尤为重要，其工作的重要性也随着各航空公司服务质量的不断提高，逐渐受到重视。一名优秀的客舱播音员不仅要有扎实的专业知识和理论基础，还要有丰富的文化和社会知识。客舱服务质量的好坏与客舱播音员有很大的关系。

一、真诚服务意识

客舱播音员首先应该用真诚的态度为旅客服务，特别是在语言服务中，只有真诚的态度才能赢得旅客的尊重、好感和信任。因而客舱播音员的职责不仅仅是播报信息，更多的是为旅客服务。客舱播音员首先是一名乘务员，其次才是客舱播音员。只有心怀服务意识，才能成为一名称职的客舱播音员。

随着经济全球化进程的加深，国内外航空公司的竞争也变得日益激烈。当今各家航空公司的竞争逐渐转向全方位的服务竞争。提升客舱播音员的服务意识对于航空公司塑造良好的形象具有现实指导意义。

空乘人员在服务过程中要增强服务意识，站在旅客的角度来思考问题，使旅客产生宾至如归的感觉是服务的最高境界。

■ 案例

经常听到女生说："我想当空姐。"是啊，那是多么好看的一群人——穿着漂亮的制服，拖着箱子排成一排，娉娉婷婷走在机场的长廊里……可真正成为一名空中乘务员是很不容易的，初试、复试、英语口试、笔试、政审、体检……层层筛选。如今的空乘人员，已然和大家印象中的空姐不一样了，在行业逐渐走向国际化的今天，选拔空乘人员更加看重亲和力、服务意识、语言沟通能力和对紧急情况的处理能力。因为空中乘务员承担的不仅仅是端茶送水这样的基本服务，更多的是在发生紧急情况时保障旅客的安全。

直到做了乘务员，我才知道原来从事这份工作要做的事情有那么多。每天早上起床、洗漱、化妆、穿衣，拉上箱子到公司开航前准备会，上了飞机后便正式开始一天的工作。首先是检查客舱的安全设施：救生筏、急救包、灭火器、氧气瓶……确保万无一失后，要清点餐食和服务设施，旅客登机后，要进行滑梯预位、安全出口的介绍和一遍又一遍的安全检查……每项操作都有一个标准化的流程，我们需要做的，就是把每件事情按照流程做好，而这些都是为了保证安全。举个例子，为了避免发餐时因突然颠簸而导致餐车里的餐盒脱出，烫伤周围旅客或是乘务员自己，公司要求发餐时每拿出一盒餐食，就要锁闭餐车门，等上一位旅客服务完成后，再重新打开餐车门取用餐盒。平均一架飞机上有160名旅客，一个乘务员每天起起落落4次，这样的动作每天都要重复1 280次。

空乘的工作，起早贪黑，辛苦又烦琐，可它依然是人人都羡慕的工作，为什么呢？人们总说"读万卷书，不如行万里路"，而空乘，大概就是少数可以日行万里的工作之一。跟着飞机，走走停停，每到一个陌生的城市，都能看到不一样的风景，遇到新鲜有趣的人，听陌生的口音，吃当地的特色小吃，怎能让人不长见识？记得2014年年初，那是我参加工作的第四年，在执行广州—洛杉矶的航班时，我遇到一位阿姨，阿姨的女儿在洛杉矶工作，孝顺的女儿买了头等舱的机票让她来美国看看。航班刚刚进入平飞，阿姨便按了呼唤铃，我连忙走过去，发现她的脸色非常差，满头大汗，虚弱地跟我说："我要输液，给我输液。"不巧的是，那次的航班上并没有医生，联系机场和乘务长后，我来到阿姨身边，初步判断她是虚弱脱水，结果一问才知，阿姨是北方人，到广州转机，因为水土不服，上吐下泻，已经两天没进食了。于是我赶紧用砂糖和盐冲了一杯盐糖水给她喝下。或许是乘务员天生的责任感使然，那次航班，每隔两个小时，我就会送去一杯盐糖水，直到阿姨的脸色慢慢好转。最后当飞机平稳落地，地面服务人员将阿姨接走时，她坐在轮椅上不住地回头，眼里泛着泪光，而此时的我才真正意识到，作为一名乘务员，最骄傲的应该是什么。

我热爱这份工作，它给了我足够的新鲜感，也给了我助人为乐的自豪感，它能让我在两万五千英尺的高空，在不同的城市间肆意挥洒汗水和青春，不断打磨，不断历练，并最终成为自己想要成为的那个人。

（资料来源：空中乘务专业——一份远离地球表面的工作，《大学》（高考金刊）2017年第3期。）

二、扎实的专业知识及播音功底

近几年来,随着航空事业的飞速发展,人们对物质文化生活的需求不断提高,给航空运输服务行业提出了更高的要求。国内外各大航空公司纷纷采取措施增加硬件投入、强化内部管理、提高服务质量、打造品牌服务。在这样的形势下,乘务员扎实的专业知识是至关重要的。一名优秀的乘务员不仅要有扎实的专业知识,还要有丰富的文化和社会知识。而客舱播音员作为客舱服务的指导者,其工作包含从迎客到送客之间的所有服务。因此,客舱播音员的专业知识应该比普通乘务员更加扎实、丰富。

扎实的专业知识是客舱播音员必备的基本素质,要成为一名合格的客舱播音员还要注意一些播音技巧。乘务员在播音时,必须运用一些播音技巧使声音悦耳动听。播音时声音要清晰、明快清脆。要做到这些就要有扎实的播音基础。

(1)规范生活用语,纠正自己日常生活中的语音错误。不论在生活还是在飞行中,乘务员都要要求自己吐字发音准确、韵调和谐。在每次广播前要做好播音准备工作,在细节上严格要求自己,长此以往才会形成一种广播习惯。

(2)在服务过程中学会选择合适的语气、语调。面对各类服务沟通问题时,都要选择一种符合当事人心情的语气,让当事人感受到关心和理解。这样既能满足对方的心理诉求,又能完整地表达自己的意思。

(3)在与旅客交流的过程中,必须学会控制语速。一些乘务员的语速较快,在播报航空信息的时候尚可,但与旅客交流时,过快的语速就略显不当了。特别是与小孩或老年人交流时,既要注意自己的语速,还要注意自己的情感状态。

(4)在机上播音时,乘务员还应灵活掌握播音技巧。其中,包括乘务员播报航班信息的对象感、语气、重音、节奏、停连等。除了掌握以上的技巧,乘务员还要根据环境做出相应的变换。遇到特殊情况,例如播报误机、返航、取消航班、备降一类的信息时,更要注意建立对象感,运用合适的语气、节奏、停连,安抚旅客的情绪,向旅客表达歉意。

(5)在飞机遇到紧急情况时,客舱播音员甚至还要代机长广播。这时,客舱播音员首先要调整好自身的状态,把握好情感基调,不能因为自己的表达影响旅客的心情,从而引起骚乱或恐慌。

三、良好的应变能力和心理素质

心理素质是人的一种内在情感表现。飞机在飞行过程中受内外多种因素的影响,容易出现一系列的意外状况,这些意外状况具有较强的突发性,是人无法预测的,乘务人员遇到这种意外状况如果不能冷静沉着地应对,其后期工作将无法顺利开展。因此,空中乘务人员要有良好的心理素质,在遇到突发状况时能够冷静沉着地应对,并做出正确的操作。

应变能力是人内在的一种潜能。飞机在飞行过程中遇到意外状况时,飞机上的旅客会出现不同程度的慌张、紧张、焦急等情绪,此时需要空中乘务人员针对突发状况做出积极、正确的解答。播报过程中应保证语言简洁、逻辑清晰、语气平和。如果空中乘务人员缺乏良好的应变能力,客舱广播不仅无法发挥其应有的作用,反而会给旅客带来一定的负面影响。因此,空中乘务人员要具备随机应变能力,能够在突发情况发生的第一时间做好旅客的心理安抚工作。

四、涉外服务能力

现在空乘人员的外语能力也越来越受到重视。空乘英语更加强调服务人员在服务过程中准确的语言表达能力、对突发事件的紧急处理能力及良好的应变沟通能力。英语会话能力是乘务员最基本的素质之一,历来倍受重视。

乘务员在进行涉外服务时,必须注意自身的礼仪规范。第一,涉外服务时要热情大方,要时刻注意乘务员与旅客之间的关系是平等的。乘务员既要热情大方,又要不卑不亢。第二,乘务员要十分注意接待与被接待双方身份对等,尽量避免接待方身份低于被接待方的失礼行为。第三,在涉外服务接待中,乘务员必须保证接待航班的接待规格与宾客身份相符,不能怠慢外国来宾。在特殊情况下,还要安排经验更加丰富的人员进行接待。第四,乘务员在接待外国来宾时,要时刻注意握手、打招呼、交谈、入座等细节。把握好细节,才能成为一个优秀的乘务员。

五、良好的沟通能力

人与人之间的交往离不开沟通,良好的沟通能力对每个乘务员来说都是至关重要的。无论是在播报信息时,还是在服务过程中,让旅客感受到诚恳的态度是极为重要的。一些乘务员的服务十分规范,业务水平比较高,但如果缺少真诚的沟通,也无法满足旅客的心理需求。

有这样一个案例,一位海外归来的老年旅客与飞机上的乘务员交谈。老人问乘务员:"你是什么地方的人啊?"乘务员回答:"南京人"。老人又问:"你熟悉南京吗?"乘务员谦虚地说:"基本的我还是知道的。"他又问:"南京是六朝古都,是哪六朝啊?"乘务员很有礼貌地回答了。老人又问道:"明朝为什么迁都北京?"这个问题确实难倒了乘务员,乘务员很抱歉地回答不知道。老人笑着说:"没关系,你很诚实。"其实,人与人之间沟通最重要的就是真诚,遇到自己不清楚的问题要如实相告,这是乘务员要遵守的基本原则。

乘务员在播报信息的过程中,无须与旅客进行面对面的交流,仅需利用话筒完成信息的播报任务,这种播报方式容易拉开乘务员与旅客之间的距离。为此,乘务员需要树立以人为本的服务意识,从旅客的角度出发,了解旅客在乘坐航班时的内在需求,将旅客真正关注的内容通过客舱广播的形式传达给旅客。

任务三　客舱播音技巧训练

对乘务员来说,客舱广播尤为重要。大部分旅客都盼望着在旅途中能够听到乘务员温

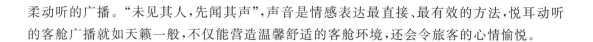

柔动听的广播。"未见其人,先闻其声",声音是情感表达最直接、最有效的方法,悦耳动听的客舱广播就如天籁一般,不仅能营造温馨舒适的客舱环境,还会令旅客的心情愉悦。

一、广播发音技巧

客舱播音员作为客舱服务和安全的指导者,工作内容包含航前、航中、航后、特殊情况等服务,必须把这些信息通过广播有效地传达给旅客。客舱广播是服务技能的重要组成部分,客舱广播语言得体、语音标准、语调亲切,能够确保旅客听到广播并积极配合乘务员的工作,为旅客提供优质的服务,有利于航空公司整体形象的提高。

(一)空中乘务客舱广播的外部技巧

空中乘务客舱广播的外部技巧主要包括空中乘务人员的发音、语气、语速、重音四个方面,具体表现如下。

第一,空中乘务人员发音的规范性。

语言是人际交往的基本手段,影响他人对自己的第一印象。在空中乘务客舱广播的过程中,如果乘务人员发音不标准,旅客可能会对广播内容产生认知性偏差,甚至错过一些重要信息,降低客舱广播的信息传播质量,降低旅客对空中乘务人员服务的满意度。因此,空中乘务客舱广播的主要目的是在最短的时间内,将信息准确无误地传达给每一位旅客。为保证每位旅客都能听懂乘务人员传达的内容,民航业要求每一位空中乘务人员掌握规范的普通话发音,并将规范的发音作为衡量乘务人员是否符合职业要求的基本标准。

第二,空中乘务人员语气的准确性。

掌握正确的说话语气是乘务人员在客舱广播中必备的技能之一。语气是指乘务人员在某种特定情感下展现出来的一种声音形式,乘务人员在进行客舱广播时,应控制好个人情绪,用稳定、平和的心态去应对飞机在飞行过程中遇到的各种突发情况。用热情、饱满的态度为每一位旅客提供服务,使每一位旅客都有宾至如归的感觉。播报信息时,乘务人员应保证语气平缓,口腔自然放松,语调抑扬顿挫。

第三,空中乘务人员语速的适中性。

在客舱广播的过程中,乘务人员播报信息的语速过快或过慢都会给旅客带来不适的感觉,因此乘务人员在每一段信息播报中,都要保证语速适中。若遇到紧急情况,乘务人员在播报时可以适当加快语速,但不可因紧张导致语速过快,给旅客带来慌乱、紧张的感觉。为此,乘务人员应时刻保持冷静沉着的工作态度,根据播报内容,科学调整说话的语速,用简洁明了的语言将信息传达给旅客,并在客舱广播的过程中做好客舱秩序的维护工作。

第四,空中乘务人员重音的科学性。

重音是指人在说话时将某个音阶凸显出来。空中乘务人员在广播过程中,想要将信息的层次关系和语义轻重关系传达给旅客,就需要正确把握播报内容,突出情感表达,强化语义,处理好重音。在信息播报过程中,若信息中的数字或文字反复出现,乘务员需要根据其所在的语境及重要性进行判断,明确哪些信息需要使用重音强调,哪些无须强调。

（二）空中乘务客舱广播的内部技巧

空中乘务客舱广播的内部技巧主要是指空中乘务人员良好的心理素质、灵活的随机应变能力以及与旅客之间的情感交流。具体表现如下。

1. 建立客舱广播的对象感

乘务员在播报信息的过程中，需要提升与旅客之间的交流感，如果不重视旅客的心理需求，只是简单地在话筒前完成播报任务，容易导致与旅客缺乏交流的亲密感。客舱广播是在用语言传达情感，这就要求乘务员在客舱播音过程中首先要建立对象感，即在客舱播音时要设想面对着旅客，考虑旅客的心理要求、愿望和情绪等，并调动自己的思想感情。

乘务员要树立以人为本服务的理念，站在旅客的角度去思考问题，了解旅客的内在需求。在短暂的航行过程中，及时播报与航班相关和旅客关心的信息，并对自己的播报情况进行反思，多揣摩旅客的心理，创造类似双方交流的语言环境，高效有序地完成飞行中的广播服务。另外，旅客的文化水平存在一定差异，这就要求乘务员在播报时要注重语言的逻辑和层次性，以免给旅客的理解造成困难。

2. 把握客舱广播时的情感

要用心为旅客服务，需要用情感搭建与旅客沟通的桥梁。客舱广播要通过声音展示乘务员专业、温馨、有责任感的服务形象，打造高端、热情的客舱服务体验。这要求乘务员应将广播词由死板地"念"，变成富有感情地"说"。

例如，播报服务类内容时，声音要温婉灵悦，让人如饮甘饴，心情愉悦；在播报安全类和应急撤离信息时，声音则要情感适中，传递出沉稳和专业的感觉。面对飞行途中的突发状况时，乘务员应该沉着冷静，及时安抚旅客，做到临危不惧，向旅客即时播报相关信息，切不可引起旅客的恐慌。

（三）英语语音规范

掌握英语语音知识、发音规范、吐词清晰，是客舱广播的基础。例如，"red wine"中的"red"读元音/e/时，不能受母语或方言干扰，不能用汉语的"爱"来代替/e/。"thank"中字母组合"th"所发的音与"soup"中的"s"的发音不同，在汉语语音中没有类似"th"的发音，发音时，舌端靠近上齿背面，气流经舌端和上齿背面摩擦成音。"travel"中字母"v"所发的音是唇齿摩擦的浊辅音，发音时需要下唇轻触上齿，气流经唇齿间空隙摩擦成音，汉语里也没有对应的发音，不能读成英文字母"w"的发音/w/。英语的辅音在单独发音或拼读时只能发它的本音，因此，"chicken soup"中的"soup"不能读成/suːpu/，不能在辅音后添加元音。

播音时，如果忽略重音，也会影响播音质量，甚至导致交际失败。英语有单音节词、双音节词或多音节词，在读多音节单词，如"recommend"和"electronic"时，可能会受汉语母语负迁移的影响，不能区分轻重音节。重读音节要读得长些、慢些，因而显得特别响亮清楚。

句子中的实词一般要求重读,实词包括名词、动词、代词、形容词和副词等,如在句子"We apologize for the delay due to air traffic control, and we thank you for your understanding and cooperation"里,"apologize""air traffic control""understanding""cooperation"需要重读。虚词一般不重读,非重读音节要读得快些、短些,不必清楚响亮。逻辑重音是通过重读来强调要表达的内容,比如,"Your carry-on items are securely stowed in the overhead bin or under the seat in front of you",这个句子里的"overhead""under"要重读,需要强调位置,告知旅客。因此,句子的重音并不是一成不变的,播音时要根据播音内容来把握。

1 连读与停顿

播报时还要学会连读,第一个单词末的辅音要和第二个单词首的元音连读,如"check in""flight attendant"。在读"a member of"时,"member"以"r"结尾,后一个单词"of"是以元音/ə/开头,这时"r"要与后面的元音/ə/拼起来连读。另外,英语中的六个爆破音"b、p、d、t、g、k",当任何两个字母相邻时要连读,比如在读"upright position""ground temperature"时,t,d发不完全爆破音,只需做出发音的准备,但并不发音,稍停顿后发后面的爆破音p,t。只有掌握连读发音技巧,英语播音才会更地道。

为了让旅客听明白广播所要表达的意思,当句子较长需要换气时,就要停顿断句,让旅客有效接受信息。由于语言的差异,播音员在进行英语播音时往往缺乏"意群"节奏感,因此播音员平时要加强训练,学会划分意群,学会停顿。有标点符号的地方要停顿,意群之间,即词组、短语、从句之间也要停顿。比如,"Please make sure/that your mobile phones/and other electronic devices,/including those with flight mode,/are powered off",这里"/"表示停顿。正确的播音还要注意语速,学会控制语速的快慢。播音员在播音前需要充分备稿,提前理解句子和篇章的内容,这样就不容易出现断句增加或减少、播读时间延长或缩短等问题。

例:Ladies and gentlemen,/good morning,/welcome aboard/this inaugural flight/from TJ to SH./We are very glad/to serve you. The air distance/is/1133 kilometers,our flying time/is/1 hour/and 45 minutes. At this time,/please make sure/that your seat belt is fastened/and refrain from smoking/during the whole flight.

2 语调升降起伏

英语的基本语调分为升调和降调。汉语中很少用升调,播音员要形成运用升调的习惯。

语调就是一句话里语音高低轻重快慢的配置,表示一定的语气和情感。语调是影响旅客听辨能力的一个重要因素。不同的语调表达不同的语意,升降的过程可以是急促的,也可以是缓慢的。选择性短语或并列短语的前半部分用升调;表达完整的或肯定的含义时用降调,句子结尾一般用降调。说话人可以通过语调准确地表达各种信息。

(1)升调。升调多用来表示"不肯定"和"未完结"的意思,比如:一般疑问句、语气委婉的祈使句,以及用陈述句表示疑问的各类句子。如:

①Shall I tell him to come and see you?(一般疑问句)

②You like him?(用陈述句表达疑问的句子,期待得到对方证实)

（2）降调。降调表示"肯定"和"完结"。一般用于陈述句、特殊疑问句、命令句和感叹句中。例如

①Swimming is my favorite.（用于陈述句，表示肯定的意义）

②What did you find there?（用于特殊疑问句，表示说话人浓厚的兴趣）

③Tell me all about it.（用于语气较强的命令）

④How nice!（用于感叹句，表示感叹）

例如，Ladies↗ and gentlemen↘, welcome aboard China Southern Airlines↘, a member of SkyTeam↘，这里"↗"表示升调，"↘"表示降调。正确使用语调，客舱英语广播才会听起来抑扬顿挫、清晰悦耳。

例：Good morning↗, ladies and gentlemen↘, I am Li Ping↗, your chief purser↘. On behalf of Air China Airlines↘, we extend the most sincere greetings to you↗ and members of our Phoenix Club↘. It's a pleasure to see you again↘. Our team is looking forward to making a safe↗ and pleasant journey↘. Thank you.↘

英语中除了升调、降调这两种基本的语调外，还有降升调、升降调、平调等。我们掌握了基本的升降调后，可以通过大量阅读增加语感。

（四）广播要有情感投入

客舱广播应该以旅客为中心，如果播音员广播时心中没有旅客，只是为了完成工作任务，语言就会变得平淡生硬、缺乏亲和力。如果播音员心中装着旅客，能感受旅客的情绪，信息就会被清晰有效地传播。"欢迎广播"要求热情洋溢、亲切，"落地广播"要求沉稳、安心、得体，给旅客宾至如归的感觉。播报安全带、救生衣等内容时要形象生动，使旅客大脑中再现这些情景。播报特殊情况时，乘务员要调整心态，把握情感基调，根据环境情况变化，灵活变换播音技巧，沉着冷静，安抚旅客的情绪，不能因为自己错误的播音方式给旅客带来恐慌。播音语言要有表现力和感染力，达到情感与声音的统一。语言能力不等于播音技巧。播音技巧的提高不是一朝一夕之事，必须经过专业指导和大量训练才能达到理想的效果。

二、广播能力培养

（一）语速的把握

语速即具体单位时间内所播报的字数。客舱服务型的广播，一般要求为中速，即每分钟200个汉字，广播时间要严格控制。客舱广播的停顿应该是在句与句之间，而不是字与字之间，广播得太快，听者会觉得焦虑；广播得太慢，听者会觉得烦闷，所以播音员需要反复练习，严格把控广播时间，不可过快或过慢。

（二）把握代入感

客舱广播的沟通对象是旅客，让旅客听得舒服才是最终目的，想要使广播悦耳动听必须加入自己的情感，使播报内容情景化。

在广播词中，会出现设施介绍、物品使用、风景介绍等，这些在播音员的脑海里应该像"过电影"那样形成连续不断的画面。例如，当播音员在广播"如果客舱失压，氧气面罩会自动脱落，氧气面罩脱落后请用力向下拉面罩，将面罩罩在口鼻处进行正常呼吸"时，播音员的脑海中应该有客舱失压时氧气面罩脱落的场景，还要有氧气面罩脱落后用力向下拉面罩的这个动作。所以，播音员在处理广播稿件时，不仅要认识稿件的字面内容，还要用心感受文字蕴含的情感。

将具体的场景通过有声语言表现出来是客舱播音员在客舱播音过程中调动思想感情，使感情与思维处于活跃状态的一种手段。情景再现在客舱广播中具有特定的含义，即在客舱服务与客舱安全管理的前提下，播音员对客舱广播词的具体内容进行联想，使广播词中的具体物品、服务项目等在广播员脑海中浮现，并形成连续不断的画面，从而引发播音员内在情感和外在表达的思维过程。

情景再现中有三个关键点：感受、想象、表达。它们之间的关系是：感受是基础，想象是桥梁，表达是实现。换句话说，我们要掌握情景再现这一有声语言的表达技巧，需要具备三种能力：感受力、想象力和表达力。

人是通过灵敏的感觉器官和文字语言来获取外界信息的。我们在客舱里通过我们灵敏的感觉器官，把外界接收的信息储存在我们的大脑里，我们的感觉器官受到了外界的刺激，就会把这些刺激通过神经传导到大脑皮层，在大脑皮层留下一些印记，这就是感觉。感觉是认识事物的第一步，是非常宝贵的，它是非常形象、非常具体的，有时也非常深刻。

文字是有声语言的符号，我们阅读文字时，会自然地联系自己的生活阅历，然后产生想象和联想。我们在阅读、表达和倾听时，会随着文字与声音的描述，在脑海中出现一个又一个连续不断的活动画面，就像看到了稿件描写的人和物、情和景，就像看到了事件发生、发展的全过程。同时，这也引发了人的思想感情的起伏变化，这就是感受。当我们说起具体的客舱设施和事物时，我们的脑海中应该产生相应的具体实物的画面，我们就是要通过有声语言把自己储存在脑海中的这些画面表达出来。

在对广播词的具体认知中，感觉器官的联系是密切的、明显的，感觉器官所感受到的外界实物是要和具体的情感相结合的。要播好客舱广播词，就要感受稿件描写的人物、情境等种种形象和事情发生、发展的过程。

想象是人对大脑里已储存的东西进行加工改造，形成新形象的心理过程，是一种特殊的思维形式。想象与思维都属于高级的认知过程，并且二者有着密切的联系。想象通常是根据自己的阅历对具体实物进行重新排列组合的过程，这种想象不根据现成的描述，而是大脑独立产生新形象的过程。

广播词的明确性使得播音员的想象不能随意，每一篇广播词都已规定想象的目的、性质。这种想象必须以符合客舱广播词的需要为前提，以客舱广播词提供的内容为原型。

播音员在注重具体事物感受的同时，还要注意广播词在结构上的整体逻辑关系。广播词越具体越好。它越具体，描述具体情境的每一个环节就越清楚，这样也形成了表达的整体性。有的播音员虽然脑海里有了具体的画面、有了具体的情境，但整体的表达缺乏真情实感，这也是不行的。我们要把广播词所表述的具体内容当作亲身经历一样，把自己融入具体的事件、场景中去，只有这样才能更好地把握技巧，播好客舱广播。

（三）微笑广播

服务意识的本质在于它是乘务员发自内心的，也是乘务员的一种本能反应和习惯。乘务员服务时的一举一动，旅客都看在眼里。乘务员是按程序、按规定完成基本工作，还是用心为旅客提供帮助，旅客心如明镜。微笑是发自内心还是生硬、不自然的职业表情，旅客都能感受到。所以乘务员没有强烈的服务意识，在激烈的市场竞争中是很难赢得更多回头客的。

广播传递微笑，服务类广播必须达到"未见其人，听其声，知其行"的效果，让旅客未见人就能感受到乘务员的热情。心理学家认为，在人的所有表情中，微笑是最坦荡和最有吸引力的。微笑是服务人员美好心灵和友好态度的外在表现，是与客人交流沟通的美好桥梁。在服务中，要对旅客主动微笑，自然大方地微笑，让微笑服务成为习惯。

项目小结

客舱服务包括礼仪、沟通、卫生、广播、救助、餐饮、娱乐、咨询等方面。客舱服务一般包含三个阶段：上机前准备阶段、机上准备阶段、空中服务实施阶段。

空乘服务语言要求普通话标准流利，语言服务要真诚亲切，服务语言要巧妙，能运用外语流利沟通。

客舱广播是指服务过程中，空中乘务员借助一定的词汇、语气、语调表达思想、感情、意愿，与旅客进行交流的一种比较规范又比较灵活的沟通方式。其内容包括航班的航程、时间、航线地理、旅游景点、餐饮娱乐等方面的信息，还有以安全演示、安全提醒和紧急状况疏导为内容的客舱广播。客舱广播有柔和、清晰、纯正、言简意赅等特点。其内容结构包含开场白、主体部分和结束语三部分。

客舱广播是空中乘务员内在修养和心态素质的外化，客舱播音考察的不是乘务员的播音方法、技巧，而是乘务员的综合素养和能力。

民航客舱播音员要有真诚服务意识、扎实的专业知识及播音功底、良好的应变能力和心理素质、涉外服务能力和良好的沟通能力等。

客舱广播要求空中乘务员在外在方面要做到发音的规范性、语气的准确性、语速的适中性、重音的科学性。内在方面要有良好的心理素质，能够在遇到突发状况时，冷静沉着地应对，并做出正确的操作。要有随机应变能力，能够在突发情况发生的第一时间做好旅客的心理安抚工作。

客舱服务广播要有情感投入。需要反复练习，严格把控时间，把握情境代入感，开展微笑服务。

项目训练

1. 在飞往广州的航班上,部分旅客感到有些口渴,向乘务员询问是否有茶水饮料。假如你是乘务员,应如何对旅客进行餐前广播?

2. 分小组按情境拟写广播词,模仿乘务员和不同旅客。每小组在模拟时,其他小组要认真观看,并做好记录。然后根据民航广播播音用语的基本要求进行自我评价,并与其他小组进行互评。

项　　目	考核要点	完成情况	评定等级
客舱广播	播报及时		
	播报语气适当		
	广播词格式符合规范		
	广播词表达准确		
	语音音量适中		
	语调生动		
综合评定等级			

3. 小组合作,自设情境(起飞安全提醒、飞机颠簸时、即将发放午餐等)并合理运用客舱广播用语,拍成视频,上传班级 QQ 群中。

4. 社会上普遍存在对空中乘务员工资高的羡慕,如果你被问及工资高的原因,你会怎么回答?

项目二　机上服务广播常用词汇和表达

项目目标

- **知识目标**
  了解机上服务广播的基础单词和短语。
- **能力目标**
  通过学习与机上服务广播相关的单词和短语,掌握基本知识要点。
- **素质目标**
  掌握机上服务的基础知识,提高个人服务能力。

知识框架

```
机上服务广播常用词汇和表达
├── 任务一 机场广播常用词汇和表达
├── 任务二 客舱服务广播常用词汇和表达
├── 任务三 客舱安全广播常用词汇和表达
└── 任务四 机场主要设施词汇
```

任务一　机场广播常用词汇和表达

announce	[əˈnaʊns]	v. 宣布;通告
passenger	[ˈpæsɪndʒə]	n. 旅客
proceed	[prəʊˈsiːd]	v. 进行;前进
proceed to		继续下去;前往
attention	[əˈtenʃn]	n. 注意;注意力
departure	[dɪˈpɑːtʃə]	n. 离开;起程
boarding	[ˈbɔːdɪŋ]	v. 上(船、车或飞机)
check-in		n. 签到;办理乘机手续

续表

commencement	[kəˈmensmənt]	n. 开始
flight	[flaɪt]	n. 飞行；航班
be postponed		使延迟，推迟
boarding pass		登机牌
go through		通过
security check		安检
disembark	[ˌdɪsɪmˈbɑːk]	v. 登陆（上岸）
terminal building	[ˈtɜːmɪnl]	候机楼

任务二　客舱服务广播常用词汇和表达

article	[ˈɑːtɪkl]	n. 物品
item	[ˈaɪtəm]	n. 条款；商品；物品
ladies and gentlemen		女士们，先生们
welcome aboard		欢迎登机
aisle	[aɪl]	n. 通道；过道
take your seat		入座
arrange	[əˈreɪndʒ]	v. 安排；整理
be dedicated to		致力于
entire crew		全体机组成员
appreciate	[əˈpriːʃieɪt]	v. 欣赏；感激
remain	[rɪˈmeɪn]	v. 保持；停留
inconvenience	[ˌɪnkənˈviːnjəns]	n. 不便，麻烦
according to		根据
on the edge of		在……的边缘
in front of		在……前面
air conditioning system		空调系统
pleasure	[ˈpleʒə]	n. 乐趣
overhead compartment		行李架
prior to		在……之前
take off		起飞
regret for		对……感到抱歉；对……表示遗憾
fasten	[ˈfɑːsn]	v. 系上；扣住

续表

code-share flight		代码共享航班
route	[ruːt]	n. 路线；航线
province	[ˈprɒvɪns]	n. 省
recommend	[ˌrekəˈmend]	v. 推荐；介绍
assistance	[əˈsɪstəns]	n. 援助，帮助
cooperation	[kəʊˌɒpəˈreɪʃən]	n. 合作
salutatory	[səˈluːtətərɪ]	adj. 致意的，欢迎的；n. 祝词，开幕词
spare no effort to		尽最大的努力……
excellent	[ˈeksələnt]	adj. 卓越的；极好的；杰出的
catering service		餐饮服务
blanket	[ˈblænkɪt]	n. 毛毯
temperature	[ˈtemprɪtʃə]	n. 温度
latest weather report		最新天气预报
centigrade	[ˈsentɪgreɪd]	adj. 摄氏度的
discomfort	[dɪsˈkʌmfət]	n. 不适；不舒服
selection	[sɪˈlekʃən]	n. 选择；挑选
formality	[fɔːˈmælɪtɪ]	n. 正式手续；仪式
entry forms		入境表格
belongings	[bɪˈlɒŋɪŋz]	n. 财物；所有物；行李
descent	[dɪˈsent]	n. 下降
cabin pressure		客舱压力
swallow	[ˈswɒləʊ]	v. 吞下；吞咽
inform	[ɪnˈfɔːm]	v. 通知；告诉；报告
destination	[ˌdestɪˈneɪʃən]	n. 目的地；终点
taxiing	[ˈtæksɪŋ]	v. 滑行；adj. 滑行的
disembark	[ˌdɪsɪmˈbɑːk]	v. 登陆，下飞机
transit counter		中转柜台
baggage claim area		行李提取处
strive to		努力
control tower		（机场）指挥塔台
final descent		最后的降落
runway congestion		跑道拥堵
switch off		关掉，切断（电源）
communicate	[kəˈmjuːnɪkeɪt]	v. 通信；沟通
cockpit	[ˈkɒkpɪt]	n. 驾驶舱

续表

locker	[ˈlɒkə]	n. 柜；箱
brighten	[ˈbraɪtən]	v. 使……亮，调亮
boarding bridge		廊桥
shuttle bus		摆渡车
ramp	[ræmp]	n. 客梯车；斜坡
late arrival		晚点
apologize for		道歉
due to		由于
en route		在途中
deicing	[ˈdiːɪsɪŋ]	v. 除冰
air traffic control		航空管制
load	[ləʊd]	n. 负载；v. 装
flight document		随机文件
cargo	[ˈkɑːgəʊ]	n. 货物
balance	[ˈbæləns]	n. 平衡；v. 使……平衡
ground staff		地面人员
delay	[dɪˈleɪ]	v. 延误
weather condition		天气情况
estimated	[ˈestɪmeɪd]	v. 估测；估计
understanding	[ˌʌndəˈstændɪŋ]	n. 理解
medical assistance		医疗救助
identify	[aɪˈdentɪfaɪ]	v. 确定；确认
New Year's Day		元旦
Chinese Lunar New Year's Eve		春节，除夕
International Women's Day		妇女节
International Labour Day		劳动节
International Children's Day		儿童节
Army Day		建军节
Teacher's Day		教师节
Mid-Autumn Day		中秋节
National Day		国庆节
Christmas		圣诞节
prosperous	[ˈprɒspərəs]	adj. 繁荣的；兴旺的
celebration	[ˌselɪˈbreɪʃən]	n. 庆祝

任务三 客舱安全广播常用词汇和表达

单词	音标	释义
restriction	[rɪˈstrɪkʃən]	n. 限制；管制
electronic	[ˌɪlekˈtrɒnɪk]	adj. 电子的
device	[dɪˈvaɪs]	n. 装置；设备
cabin door		舱门
avoid	[əˈvɔɪd]	v. 避免
interference	[ˌɪntəˈfɪərəns]	n. 干涉
navigation system		导航系统
turn off		（把）关掉
prohibit	[prəʊˈhɪbɪt]	v. 阻止；禁止
mobile phone		移动电话
ensure	[enˈʃʊə]	v. 确保
upright position		垂直的位置
whole	[həʊl]	adj. 全部的
pleasant	[ˈplezənt]	adj. 令人愉快的
trip	[trɪp]	n. 旅程
oxygen mask		氧气面罩
life vest		救生衣
location	[ləʊˈkeɪʃən]	n. 位置
emergency exit		紧急出口
safety demonstration(video)		安全演示（视频）
store	[stɔː]	n. 商店，贮存物；v. 储存
overhead compartment		行李架
drop	[drɒp]	v. 落下
automatically	[ˌɔːtəˈmætɪklɪ]	adv. 自动地
in case of		万一
pull	[pʊl]	v. 拉
slip	[slɪp]	v./n. 滑倒
flap	[flæp]	n. 片状垂悬物；锁扣
elastic band		松紧带
breathe	[briːð]	v. 呼吸
normally	[ˈnɔːməlɪ]	adv. 正常地
securely	[sɪˈkjʊəlɪ]	adv. 安全地

续表

单词	音标	释义
release	[rɪˈliːs]	n. /v. 解除,释放
forward	[ˈfɔːwəd]	adj. /adv. 向前
rear	[rɪə]	n. 后部;adj. 后面的
ditching	[ˈdɪtʃɪŋ]	n. 水上迫降
remove	[rɪˈmuːv]	v. 脱掉
illuminated	[ɪˈluːmɪneɪtɪd]	adj. 发光的
instructed	[ɪnsˈtrʌktɪd]	adj. 得到指示的
buckle	[bʌkl]	n. 搭扣
strap	[stræp]	n. 带子
tab	[tæb]	n. 拉环
tightly	[ˈtaɪtlɪ]	adv. 紧紧地
waist	[weɪst]	n. 腰部
firmly	[ˈfɜːmlɪ]	adv. 稳固地
inflate	[ɪnˈfleɪt]	v. 使充气
blow	[bləʊ]	v. 吹
safety instruction		安全须知
refer to		适用于;参考
arise	[əˈraɪz]	v. 产生;出现
tray table		小桌板
footrest	[fʊtrest]	n. 脚凳
initial	[ɪˈnɪʃəl]	adj. 最初的
sunshade	[ˈsʌnʃeɪd]	n. 遮光板
make sure		确保
flying mode		飞行模式
including	[ɪnˈkluːdɪŋ]	v. 包括
turn off		把……关掉
non-smoking flight		全程禁烟航班
laptop	[ˈlæptɒp]	n. 便携式电脑
taxiing	[ˈtæksɪɪŋ]	v. 滑行
dimming	[ˈdɪmɪŋ]	v. (使)变暗
cabin lights		机舱灯
slight	[slaɪt]	adj. 微小的
moderate	[ˈmɒdərɪt]	adj. 中等的;温和的
severe	[sɪˈvɪə]	adj. 剧烈的
rough	[rʌf]	adj. 狂暴的;汹涌的

续表

rough air		扰动气流
turbulence	[ˈtɜːbjʊləns]	n. 颠簸
experiencing	[ɪkˈspɪərɪənsɪŋ]	v. 体验,经历
lavatory	[ˈlævətəri]	n. 卫生间
be suspended		暂停
watch out		当心
captain	[ˈkæptɪn]	n. 机长
pass through		经过,通过
minor	[ˈmaɪnə]	adj. 较小的
break out		突然发生;爆发
require	[rɪˈkwaɪə]	v. 需要;想要
calm	[kɑːm]	adj. 镇定的;平静的
affected	[əˈfektɪd]	adj. 受到影响的
request	[rɪˈkwest]	v. 要求
decompression	[ˌdiːkəmˈpreʃən]	n. 释压;失压
depressurization	[ˌdiːpreʃəraɪˈzeɪʃən]	n. 释压
immediately	[ɪˈmiːdiətlɪ]	adv. 立即;马上
attend	[əˈtend]	v. 出席;参加;陪同
instruction	[ɪnˈstrʌkʃən]	n. 指令
evacuate	[ɪˈvækjʊeɪt]	v. 撤离;疏散
chief purser		主任乘务长
necessary	[ˈnesəsəri]	adj. 必要的
handle	[ˈhændl]	v. 处理
stow	[stəʊ]	v. 装;装载
sharp	[ʃɑːp]	adj. 尖锐的
object	[ˈɒbdʒekt]	n. 物体
jewelry	[ˈdʒʊːəlrɪ]	n. 珠宝;首饰
tie	[taɪ]	n. 领带
scarf	[skɑːf]	n. 围巾,丝巾
hand luggage		手提行李
glasses	[ˈglɑːsɪz]	n. 眼镜
deaf-aid		n. 助听器
denture	[ˈdentʃə]	n. 假牙
explain	[ɪkˈspleɪn]	v. 解释,说明
brace for impact		抱紧防撞(抵御冲击)

续表

command	[kəˈmɑːnd]	v.命令,指挥
apart	[əˈpɑːt]	adj./adv.分离的;分开地
flat	[flæt]	adj./adv.水平地;平直地
lean	[liːn]	v.(使)倾斜;使斜靠
bend	[bend]	v.(使)弯曲;屈身
jolts	[dʒəʊlts]	v.(使)摇动
completely	[kəmˈpliːtlɪ]	adv.完全地
divert to		v.备降到……

任务四 机场主要设施词汇

aerodrome/airport	n.机场
alternate airfield	备用机场
control tower	控制塔台
hangar	n.机库
fuel farm	油库
emergency service	急救服务
localizer	n.航向信标台/定位信标
weather office	气象站
runway	n.跑道
taxiway	n.滑行道
parking bay	停机位置
maintenance area	维修区
terminal departure building	机场大厦/候机楼
seeing-off deck	送客台
international departure building	国际航班出港大厦
domestic departure lobby	国内航线出港候机厅
coffee shop	咖啡店
special waiting room	特别休息室
quarantine	v./n.检疫
customs	n.海关
emigration control	出境检查
snack bar	快餐店

续表

English	中文
automatic door	自动出入门
arrival lounge	到达大厅
departure lounge	离港大厅
transit lounge	过站大厅
telephone/telegram/fax room	电话/电报/传真间
stand-by ticket counter	补票处
flight information board	航班显示板
check-in counter	办理登机手续柜台
transfer correspondence	中转柜台
carousel	旋转行李传送带
public address	公共广播
dispatch office	签派室
police office	机场公安局(警察局)
body temperature scanner	体温检测仪
medical centre	医疗中心
escalator	自动扶梯
elevator	(升降式)电梯
moving/automatic walkway	自动步道
air bridge	登机廊桥
airport fire service	机场消防队
catering department	配餐供应部门
duty-free shop	免税商店
airport hotel	机场宾馆
VIP room	贵宾室
main lobby	主厅
freight building/cargo centre	货运大厦/货运中心
security centre	安全中心
imports shop	进口商品店
entrance	入口
passenger route	旅客通道
boarding gate No. 18	第18号登机口
boarding gate besides No. 16	第16号以外登机口
lavatory	卫生间,洗手间
international arrival building	国际航班到达大厦
taxi stand	出租汽车站

续表

domestic connection counter	国内线联运柜台
exit	出口
hotel and limousine service	旅馆及机场交通服务处
limousine stand	机场交通车站
waiting room	休息室
exchange and tax payment	兑换及付税
customs personnel	海关人员
customs inspection counter	海关检查柜台
baggage claim area	行李认领区
immigration control	入境检查
plant quarantine	植物检疫
animal quarantine	动物检疫
connection counter	联运柜台
arrival lobby	入境旅客休息室
security counter	安检柜台
security check station	安全检查站
airport tax sales	机场税购买柜台
passport control	护照检查柜台

项目三　起飞前服务广播

知识目标

　　了解起飞前广播词的内涵和用途；
　　了解起飞前基本广播词的核心要素；
　　了解如何导入起飞前基本广播词。

能力目标

　　通过对起飞前常见广播词理论知识的学习，端正服务态度，培养民航服务意识，做好对客服务的心理准备、思想准备和行为准备。

素质目标

　　掌握广播词语言的规范要求，提高自身文明修养。

知识框架

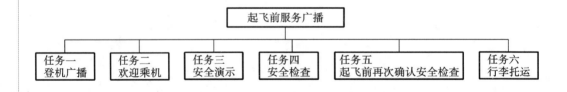

 任务一　登机广播

一、常用词汇和表达

purser　n. 乘务长
captain　n. 机长
vegetarian　n. 素食者
announcement　n. 广播词
medical　adj. 医学的

pre-flight briefing　航前准备会
aircraft type　机型
estimated flight time　预计飞行时间
flight route　飞行路线
departure time　出发时间,离港时间
estimated time of arrival　预计抵达时间
cabin service　客舱服务
passenger information　旅客信息
first class　头等舱
business class　商务舱
economy class　经济舱
special passenger　特殊旅客

二、句型练习

1. Would you like me to hang up your overcoat for you?
您要我帮您把大衣挂起来吗?
2. Please take your passport out of your luggage.
请把护照从行李里拿出来。
3. Would you mind stowing your bag in the overhead locker?
您介意把您的包放在头顶的储物柜里吗?
4. Please put your baggage under the seat or into the overhead compartment.
请把您的行李放在座位下面或放在头顶的行李舱里。
5. Would you please check if you have any valuables in your pockets?
请您检查一下口袋里有没有贵重物品好吗?
6. Your luggage is far too heavy and won't fit into the overhead compartment.
您的行李太重了,放不进头顶的行李舱。
7. If you don't mind, I'll hang the coat in the wardrobe compartment for you.
如果您不介意的话,我帮您把外套挂在衣柜的隔间里。

三、对话练习

1

PAX:Hello! Where can I get the 10:20 flight to Singapore? 您好! 请问 10:20 飞往新加坡的飞机在哪登机?

CA:Wait a moment, let me have a look. Gate 70. 请等一下,让我查查。是 70 号登机口。

PAX:Where is the gate 70? 70 号登机口在哪里?

CA:It's on the downstairs. You go downstairs and then you should go straight. Follow the sign and you will find it.

在楼下,您下楼然后直走,沿着指示牌走就能找到了。

PAX:Thanks. Could I ask another question? 谢谢。我能再问个问题吗?

CA:Yes,please. 可以。

PAX:You know that the weather is bad these days. Is there an possibility that the flight would be put off?

您知道,最近天气不是很好,航班有可能被延误吗?

CA:Sorry,I don't know. But I haven't received any notice. 对不起,我不清楚,我还没有接到任何通知。

PAX:I catch the time. I have an important meeting in Singapore. 我得赶时间,我在新加坡有一个很重要的会议要开。

CA:Don't worry. It will be fine. 别担心,会顺利的。

2

CA:Excuse me,sir.

乘务员:打扰了,先生。

PAX:Yes?

旅客:怎么了?

CA:I'm afraid I have to put your baggage in other places.

乘务员:恐怕我得把您的行李放到其他地方了。

PAX:Why? It's not in anyone's way.

旅客:为什么? 这不会妨碍任何人。

CA:No,but it might be. You're sitting next to the emergency exit. According to the airlines regulations,passengers are requested to keep the emergency exit seats clear of all baggage.

乘务员:不,可能会妨碍。您坐在紧急出口旁边。根据航空公司的规定,紧急出口座位不应该有行李。

PAX:So where could I put it? I'll need it during the flight.

旅客:那我应该把它放在哪里呢? 我需要它。

CA:Don't worry. Let me assist you with your baggage and put it into other overhead locker.

乘务员:别担心。让我帮您拿行李,把它放到头顶的行李箱里。

PAX:All right. Thank you.

旅客:好的。谢谢!

3

PAX:Excuse me,Miss. Can I put my baggage in the galley?

旅客:打扰一下,小姐。我可以把行李放到厨房里吗?

CA:I'm afraid you can't. We'll be working in the galley preparing the dinner. Besides,we'll stow litter bags there after dinner. Would you mind putting it somewhere else?

乘务员:恐怕您不能。我们将在厨房里准备晚餐。另外,晚饭后我们会把垃圾袋放在那里。您介意把它放到别的地方吗?

PAX:But my baggage is too big to go into the compartment or under my seat.

旅客:但是我的行李太大了,放不进行李舱或座位下面。

CA:Well,if you don't mind,I'll keep it safe somewhere else.

乘务员:嗯,如果您不介意的话,我会把它保管到别处。

PAX:Well,but there are some fragile items in it.

旅客:嗯,但是里面有一些易碎物品。

CA:I see. I'll keep it with care.

乘务员:我明白了。我会小心保管的。

PAX:Thank you!

旅客:谢谢!

4

CA:Pardon me for interrupting you,Madam. Your baggage is far too heavy and won't fit into the overhead compartment. It might easily fall down in case of turbulence and hurt someone.

乘务员:请原谅我打断您,女士。您的行李太重了,放不进头顶的行李箱。万一遇到颠簸,它很容易掉下来伤到人。

PAX:I see. What can I do with it?

旅客:我明白了。我该怎么做?

CA:I'm afraid you need to put it under the seat in front of you.

乘务员:您需要把它放在您前面的座位下面。

PAX:All right.

旅客:好的。

CA:Please allow me to assist you with it.

乘务员:请让我帮助您。

PAX:Thank you!

旅客:谢谢!

(The cabin attendant helps the passenger carry the bag down from the locker. Suddenly,some fruits run out of the bag.)

(客舱服务员帮旅客把袋子从储物柜里拿下来,突然,袋子里的一些水果滚落出来。)

CA:Excuse me,Madam. I'm afraid you can't take those fruits with you on this international flight. According to the quarantine requirements of Canadian government,all entry passengers to Canada are not allowed to bring in fruits.

乘务员:打扰一下,女士。您不能把这些水果带上这趟国际航班。根据加拿大政府的检疫要求,所有入境旅客都不允许携带水果。

PAX:Oh,dear. What am I supposed to do now?

旅客:哦,天哪。我现在该怎么办?

CA:Don't worry,Madam. You can choose to dispose of them by yourself,or you can give them to us,we'll be happy to be at your service.

乘务员:别担心,女士。您可以选择自己处理,也可以交给我们,我们很乐意为您服务。

PAX:Thanks. That's very nice of you.

旅客:谢谢。你真是太好了。
CA:It's a pleasure. Wish you a pleasant journey.
乘务员:这是我的荣幸。祝您旅途愉快。

四、广播词

Announcements for Boarding(登机广播)

1

Ladies and gentlemen,

May I have your attention please? Flight _____ alternated to _____ is boarding. Would you please have your belongings and boarding passes ready and board the aircraft through Gate No. _____. We wish you a pleasant journey. Thank you.

前往_____的旅客请注意:您乘坐的_____次航班现在开始登机。请您带好您的随身物品,出示登机牌,在_____号登机口登机。祝您旅途愉快。谢谢!

2

Good morning/afternoon/evening,ladies and gentlemen,

Welcome aboard Star Airlines Flight ST5237 from Shanghai to Beijing. The aircraft is Airbus 320.

Please make sure your luggage is stored in the overhead compartment or under the seat in front of you. Please keep the aisles and the exits clear, and we will assist you if you need any help.

Thank you for your cooperation!

女士们、先生们,早上/下午/晚上好!

欢迎您乘坐星星航空公司 ST5237 次航班从上海前往北京。本架飞机机型为空客 320。

请将您的手提物品放在头顶的行李架上或您前面的座椅下,请保持过道和紧急出畅通。如果您需要帮助,我们会尽快协助您。

谢谢您的合作!

3

Good morning, ladies and gentlemen,

We are honored to welcome you aboard Air China, a proud Star Alliance member. Kindly store all your carry-on luggage securely in the overhead compartment or under the seat in front of you. Please take your assigned seats as quickly as possible and leave the aisle clear for others to be seated.

We appreciate your cooperation. Thank you!

女士们、先生们,早上好!

欢迎您乘坐中国国际航空公司的航班,中国国际航空公司是星空联盟成员。请将您所有的手提行李存放在行李架上或您前面的座椅下方。找到座位的旅客,请您尽快入座,以方便后面的旅客登机。谢谢您的合作!

Announcement Made After Cabin Door Closed(舱门关闭后广播)

Ladies and gentlemen,

The cabin door is closed. For your safety, please do not use your mobile phones and certain electronic devices on board at any time. Laptop computers may not be used during the take-off and landing. Please ensure that your mobile phone is turned off. This is a non-smoking flight, please do not smoke on board.

Thank you for your cooperation.

女士们、先生们：

舱门已关闭。为了您的安全，请不要在飞机上使用您的手机和某些电子设备。在起飞和着陆过程中不能使用笔记本电脑，请确保您的手机已关闭。这是禁烟航班，请您不要在飞机上抽烟，谢谢您的合作。

Announcement for Electronic Devices Restrictions(限制使用电子设备广播)

Ladies and gentlemen,

Please note certain electronic devices must not be used on board at any time. These devices include cellular phones, AM/FM radios, televisions and remote control equipment.

All other electronic devices including laptop computers and CD players must not be switched on until fifteen minutes after take-off and must be switched off when the seat belt signs come on for landing.

Your cooperation will be much appreciated.

女士们、先生们：

请注意，任何时候都不得在飞机上使用某些电子设备。这些电子设备包括手机、AM/FM 收音机、电视和遥控设备。

其他电子设备，包括笔记本电脑和 CD 播放器，只能在起飞后十五分钟后使用，并且必须在飞机着陆安全带标志亮起时关闭。

Exercise(练习)

1. Please fill in the blanks with the appropriate words.

(1) Can I take a look at your _____ pass, sir?

(2) I prefer a _____ seat when taking an airplane, because I enjoy the beautiful views outside.

(3) The red seats in a bus are for the _____ and the senior.

2. Please fill in the blanks with the exact words or phrases according to the first letter.

Online Check-in

Do you still check in at the a _____ check-in counter? Do you know others have already enjoyed the c _____ of online check-in?

Online check-in is the process in which passengers c _____ their presences on a flight through the I _____ and print their own b _____ pass. Depending on the carrier and the s _____ flight, passengers may also enter details such as meal o _____ and baggage quantities and select their preferred seating.

This service r _____ the time a passenger would normally spend at and airport check-in counter. If a passenger needs to continue the check-in process at the a _____ after finishing an online check-in, a special l _____ is typically offered to them to reduce w _____ time. Airlines may use the system because self-service is frequently more efficient.

任务二 欢迎乘机

一、常用词汇和表达

boarding pass/boarding card 登机牌
food trolley 送餐车
lavatory 盥洗室，洗手间，厕所
Welcome aboard 欢迎登机
prohibited item 违禁物品
flight number 航班号
turbulence 湍流，颠簸
direct flight 直飞
airsickness 晕机
blanket 毛毯
emergency exit 紧急出口
passenger manifest 旅客名单
delay 延误
recline the seat 座椅后倾
departure time 起飞时间
window seat 靠窗座位
aisle seat 靠过道座位

二、句型练习

1. Our estimated time of arrival at Shanghai Pudong International Airport is 10:30 p.m.. The time now is 8:20 p.m..

我们的飞机预计在晚间 10 点 30 分到达，现在是北京时间晚间 8 点 20 分。

2. To ensure the flight safety, please make sure that your mobile phones, including

flight mode are powered off.

为了保证飞行安全,请您确认您的手机及"飞行模式"已经关闭。

3. This is a non-smoking flight. Please do not smoke during the entire flight.

本次航班全程禁止吸烟!

4. Thank you for your support and concern.

谢谢您的支持与关心!

5. We will be very happy to assist you. Thank you.

我们将非常乐意帮助您。谢谢。

6. To ensure a good rest for you during the long journey, we will dim the cabin lights.

为你确保您在旅途中得到良好的休息,我们将调暗客舱灯光。

7. For passengers who wish to read, please switch on the reading lights located above you.

想要阅读的旅客,请打开位于您上方的阅读灯。

8. We strongly recommend you to keep your seat belt fastened through the flight.

我们强烈建议您在整个飞行过程中系好安全带。

9. Because your safety is our primary concern.

您的安全是我们最关心的。

三、对话练习

1

CA:Good morning, sir. What can I do for you?

乘务员:早上好先生。有什么需要我帮助的吗?

PAX:I don't know where I can find my seat.

旅客:我不知道我的座位在哪里。

CA:Can you tell me your seat number, please?

乘务员:您能告诉我您的座位号吗?

PAX:It's 30F.

旅客:30F。

CA:It'll be five rows up on the left, the window seat. Follow me lease. Can I help you taking your bag?

乘务员:往前走5排左边靠窗座位。请跟我来!要我帮您拿行李吗?

PAX:Thank you.

旅客:谢谢。

CA:You're welcome.

乘务员:不客气。

2

CA:Good morning, Miss. Welcome aboard.

乘务员:早上好,小姐。欢迎登机。

PAX：Good morning. Where can I find my seat?

旅客：早上好。我在哪里可以找到我的座位?

CA：Could you show me your boarding pass, Miss?

乘务员：小姐,请出示您的登机牌好吗?

PAX：OK. Here you are.

旅客：好的。给你。

CA：It's 14F, it is a window seat. This way, please.

乘务员：14F,是靠窗的座位。请这边走。

PAX：Thank you!

旅客：谢谢你!

四、广播词

女士们、先生们：

欢迎您乘坐中国_____航空公司_____航班,由_____前往_____(中途降落_____)。由_____至_____的飞行距离是_____,预计空中飞行时间是_____小时_____分。飞行高度_____米,飞行速度平均每小时_____千米。

为了保障飞机导航及通讯系统的正常工作,在飞机起飞和下降过程中请不要使用手提式电脑,在整个航程中请不要使用手提电话、遥控玩具、电子游戏机、激光唱机和电音频接收机等电子设备。飞机很快就要起飞了,现在客舱乘务员进行安全检查。请您在座位上坐好,系好安全带,收起座椅靠背和小桌板。请您确认您的手提物品是否妥善安放在头顶上方的行李架内或座椅下方。(本次航班全程禁烟,在飞行途中请不要吸烟。)本次航班的乘务长将协同机上_____名乘务员竭诚为您提供及时周到的服务。

谢谢!

Good morning/afternoon/evening, ladies and gentlemen,

Welcome aboard _____ Airlines Flight _____ from _____ to _____ (via _____)The distance between _____ and _____ is _____ kilometers. Our flight will take _____ hours and _____ minutes. We will be flying at an altitude of _____ meters and the average speed is _____ kilometers per hour.

In order to ensure the normal operation of aircraft navigation and communication systems, electronic devices including cell phones, remete control toys, game players, CD players and can not be used throughout the flight and the laptop computers are not allowed to use during take-off and landing.

We will take off immediately, please be seated, fasten your seat belt, and make sure your seat back is straight up, your tray table is closed and your carry-on items are securely stowed in the overhead compartment or under the seat in front of you. (This is a non-smoking flight, please do not smoke on board.)

The (chief) purser _____ with all your crew members will be sincerely at your service. We hope you enjoy the flight! Thank you!

任务三 安全演示

一、常用词汇和表达

oxygen mask 氧气面罩
life vest 救生衣
location n. 位置
emergency exit 紧急出口
demonstration n. 示范
store v. 储存
compartment n. 储物柜,车厢隔间
drop v. 落下
automatically adv. 自动地
in case of 万一
pull v. 拉
slip v. 滑
elastic adj. 有弹力的
band n. 带,环
breathe v. 呼吸
normal adj. 正常的
securely adv. 牢固地,安全地
whole adj. 全部的
release v. 解除,释放
flap n. 片状垂悬物,锁扣
adjust v. 调整
necessary adj. 必要的
locate v. 位于
ditching n. 水上迫降
remove v. 脱掉
instructed v. 得到指示的
simply adv. 简单地
buckle n. 搭扣
strap n. 带子
tightly adv. 紧紧地
waist n. 腰部
tab n. 拉环,手柄

firmly   adv. 稳固地
inflate   v. 使充气
further   adj. 更进一步的
blow   v. 吹
illuminated   adj. 发光的
rear   n. 后部
guide   n. 指导，引路
arise   v. 产生，出现
refer to   适用于，参考
safety instruction   安全须知

二、句型练习

1. Can you show me again, please? I'm not quite clear.

您可以再给我演示一遍吗？我不太清楚。

2. Could you tell me how I inflate my life vest?

您能告诉我如何给救生衣充气吗？

3. Could you tell me the reason why we are not suggested inflating the life vest in cabin?

您能告诉我为什么不建议在客舱内给救生衣充气吗？

4. I'm not sure. Is the door very heavy?

我不确定。门很重吗？

5. Not at all. I have sat there many times.

一点也不介意。我在那儿坐过很多次了。

6. All you have to do is to pull the emergency oxygen mask towards you, hold it securely over your nose and mouth and breathe normally.

您要做的就是把紧急氧气面罩朝您拉过来，把它牢牢地戴在您的鼻子和嘴上，然后正常呼吸。

7. I suppose you didn't notice the life vest demonstration just now, sir.

先生，我想您刚才没有注意救生衣的演示吧。

8. You can inflate it by pulling these tabs down or you can blow into the mouthpieces.

您可以通过拉下这些手柄来给它充气，也可以对着吹气口吹气。

9. If all passengers inflate their life vests, there will be no room inside the cabin. Also, some broken metal from the aircraft may damage the life vest on the way out.

如果所有旅客都将救生衣充气，机舱内将没有空间。此外，飞机上的一些金属碎片可能会在逃生时损坏救生衣。

10. In the event of an emergency, do you think you can open the exit, Madam?

女士，万一发生紧急情况，您能打开出口吗？

11. Would you mind changing your seat for one next to the emergency exit?

您介意换一个靠近紧急出口的座位吗？

三、对话练习

1

PAX:I'm sorry,Miss,but can you show me again,please? I'm not quite clear.

旅客:对不起,小姐,您可以再给我演示一遍吗?我不太清楚。

CA:Okay. Look,all you have to do is to pull the emergency oxygen mask towards you,hold it securely over your nose and mouth and breathe normally. Now,are you clear?

乘务员:好的。您要做的就是把紧急氧气面罩朝您拉过来,把它牢牢地戴在您的口鼻处,然后正常呼吸。现在,您明白了吗?

PAX:I think so. Thank you.

旅客:我想是的,谢谢。

2

CA:Ladies and gentlemen,our plane has eight emergency exits. Please note your nearest exit.

乘务员:女士们、先生们,我们的飞机有八个紧急出口。请注意离您最近的出口。

(The fight attendant turns to a passenger sitting next to an over-wing exit)

(乘务员转向坐在机翼出口旁边的旅客)

CA:Excuse me,Madam. You are sitting next to an emergency exit.

乘务员:对不起,女士。您坐在紧急出口旁边。

PAX:Oh,yes.

旅客:哦,是的。

CA:In the event of an emergency,do you think you can open the exit,Madam?

乘务员:女士,如果发生紧急情况,您认为您可以打开出口吗?

PAX A:Hmm. I'm not sure. Is the door very heavy?

旅客:嗯,我不确定。门很重吗?

CA:Not very heavy. But if you would like to sit somewhere else. I'm sure I can arrange this for you.

乘务员:不是很重。但是如果您想坐在别的地方,我可以为您安排。

PAX A:Oh,thanks. That's very nice of you.

旅客:噢,谢谢。你真好。

(The flight attendant turns to another passenger)

(乘务员转向另一位旅客)

CA:Excuse me, sir. Would you mind changing your seat for one next to the emergency exit?

乘务员:对不起,先生。您介意换一个靠近紧急出口的座位吗?

PAX B:Not at all. I have sat there many times.

旅客:一点也不介意。我坐在那里很多次了。

CA:Thank you,sir.

乘务员:谢谢,先生。

四、广播词

Announcement for Safety Demonstration

Ladies and gentlemen,

We will now explain the use of the life vest, oxygen mask and seat belt, and show you the location of the emergency exits.

Your life vest is located under your seat, to put the vest on, slip it over your head. Fasten the buckles and pull the straps tightly around your waist. To inflate the vest, pull down firmly on the tabs, but do not inflate in the cabin. If your vest neck needs further inflation, you can pull the mouth-pieces from either side of the upper part of the vest and blow into the tubes.

Your oxygen mask is located in a compartment above your head. It will drop automatically in case of emergency. Pull the mask firmly toward yourself to start the flow of oxygen. Place the mask over your nose and mouth and slip the plastic band over your head. In a few seconds, the oxygen will again to flow.

Your seat belt contains two pieces. To fasten the belt, slip one place into the buckle and pull the belt tightly. Please keep your seat belt fastened securely when you are seated. There are _____ emergency exits on this aircraft. They are located in the front. the rear, the middle and the upper deck. In the event of an evacuation, emergency floor-lights will illuminate a darkened cabin, leading you to these exits.

The safety instruction is in the seat pocket in front of you. Please read it carefully as soon as possible.

Thank you!

女士们、先生们现在客舱乘务员向您介绍救生衣、氧气面罩、安全带的使用方法和应急出口的位置。

救生衣位于您座椅下面的口袋里。使用时取出,经头部穿好。将带子围在腰上扣好、系紧。然后打开充气阀门,但在客舱内不要充气。充气不足时,请将救生衣上部的两个人工充气管拉出,用嘴向里面充气。

氧气面罩储藏在您头顶的上方,发生紧急情况时面罩会自动脱落。氧气面罩脱落后,请用力向下拉面罩。将面罩罩在口鼻处,把袋子套在头上。几秒钟后,便可进行正常呼吸。

座椅上两条安全带,将带子插进带扣,然后拉紧。当您就座时,请系好安全带。本架飞机共有_____个应急出口,分别位于前部、后部、中部和上舱。在应急撤离时,紧急照明指示灯将照亮黑暗的地方,引导您到应急出口。

在您前方座椅的口袋里有安全说明书,请您尽早阅读。

谢谢!

Announcement for Seat Belt(系安全带广播)

Each chair has a seat belt that must be fastened when you are seated. Please keep your seat belt securely fastened during the whole flight. If needed, you may release the seat belt by pulling the flap forward. You can adjust it when necessary.

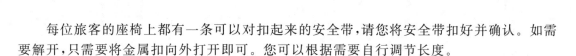

每位旅客的座椅上都有一条可以对扣起来的安全带,请您将安全带扣好并确认。如需要解开,只需要将金属扣向外打开即可。您可以根据需要自行调节长度。

Announcement for Life Vest(救生衣广播)

Your life vest is located under your seat. It can only be used in case of ditching. Please do not remove it unless instructed by your flight attendant.

To put your vest on, simply slip it over your head, then fasten the buckles and pull the straps tightly around your waist.

Upon exiting the aircraft, pull the tabs down firmly to inflate your vest, please do not inflate your vest while inside the cabin. For further inflation, simply blow into the mouth pieces on either side of your vest.

For ditching at night, a sea-light will be illuminated automatically.

救生衣在您座椅下方的口袋里,仅供水上迫降时使用,在正常情况下请不要取出。使用时取出,经头部穿好。将带子由后向前扣好,在腰间系紧。

当您离开飞机时,拉动救生衣下部的红色充气手柄,但在客舱内不要充气。充气不足时,将救生衣上部的两个充气管拉出,用嘴向里充气。

夜间迫降时,救生衣上的指示灯遇水会自动发亮。

Announcement for Emergency Exits(紧急出口广播)

There are eight(six) emergency exits. Two in the front of the cabin. two in the rear and four(two) in the middle.

The lights located on the floor will guide you to the exits if there is an emergency case. For further information, please refer to the safety instruction in the seat pocket in front of you.

Thank you.

本架飞机客舱内共有8(6)个紧急出口,前舱2个,后舱2个,中间4(2)个。客舱通道及出口处都设有紧急照明灯,紧急情况下请按指示灯路线撤离飞机。《安全须知》在您前排座椅背后的口袋里,请您在起飞前仔细阅读。谢谢!

 任务四　安全检查

一、常用词汇和表达

window shade　　n. 遮光帘
turn off　关闭
electronic device　电子设备
accessory　　n. 配件,配饰;adj. 辅助的
cell phone　手机
operation　　n. 操作

navigation　n. 航行
prohibit　v. 禁止，阻止
annoying　adj. 烦人的
call button　呼叫按钮
upright position　垂直位置
buckle　n. 搭扣，扣环
assistance　n. 帮助，援助

二、句型练习

1. The seat belt is too short for both my baby and me.
安全带对我和我的孩子来说都太短了。

2. I want to check an e-mail. It is of importance. Just a minute, all right?
我想查一封电子邮件，这封邮件对我很重要。只要一分钟，可以吗？

3. Can you show me how to return it back?
您能告诉我怎么把座椅靠背恢复到直立位置吗？

4. Can you tell me how to fasten the seat belt?
您能告诉我怎么系安全带吗？

5. Please fasten your seat belt!
请系好安全带！

6. I will bring you a baby accessory, which will make the baby feel comfortable.
我会给您拿一个婴儿辅助用品，它会使婴儿感到舒适。

7. Please turn off your cell phone.
请关掉您的手机。

8. To ensure the normal operations of the airplane navigation and communication system, cell phones are strictly prohibited on the plane.
为确保飞机导航和通信系统的正常运行，飞机上严禁使用手机。

9. You have to wait until we come to a complete stop.
您必须等到我们完全停下来。

10. Would you please return your seat back to the upright position?
请您将座椅靠背调回到直立位置好吗？

三、对话练习

1

CA: Excuse me, Madam. Please fasten your seat belt.
乘务员：对不起，女士。请系好安全带。

PAX: Oh, but I don't know how to do it. The seat belt is too short for both my baby and me.
旅客：哦，但我不知道怎么系。安全带对我和我的宝宝来说都太短了。

CA: Never mind. Let me help you. Please hold your baby outside the seat belt. I bring you a baby accessory, which will make the baby feel comfortable.

乘务员:没关系。让我来帮您。请把您的孩子抱在安全带外面。我会给您拿一个婴儿辅助用品,它会使婴儿感到舒适。

PAX:Yes. Thank you for helping me.

旅客:好的,谢谢你帮我。

2

CA:Excuse me, sir. I am sorry. Please turn off your cell phone.

乘务员:对不起,先生。我很抱歉。请关掉您的手机。

PAX:I want to check an e-mail. It is of importance. Just a minute, all right?

旅客:我想查一封电子邮件,这封邮件对我很重要。只要一分钟,可以吗?

CA:Sorry, sir. In order to ensure the normal operations of the airplane navigation and communication system, cell phone are strictly prohibited on the plane.

乘务员:对不起,先生。为了保证飞机导航和通信系统的正常运行,飞机上严禁使用手机。

PAX:Please, Miss, it is very important.

旅客:求你了,小姐,邮件很重要。

CA:Sorry, Sir. You have to wait until we come to a complete stop.

乘务员:对不起,先生。您必须等到我们完全停下来。

PAX:Oh, how annoying! What is the time now? When are we to arrive?

旅客:哦,真烦人! 现在几点了? 我们什么时候到?

CA:It is 10:30 a.m.. In about 50 minutes, we will come to a stop.

乘务员:现在是上午 10:30。大约 50 分钟后,我们将停下来。

PAX:OK. In that case, I have to wait.

旅客:好的。那样的话,我再等等。

CA:Thank you for your cooperation, Sir!

乘务员:谢谢您的合作,先生!

3

CA:Excuse me, sir. Would you please return your seat back to the upright position?

乘务员:对不起,先生。请您将座椅靠背调回到直立位置好吗?

PAX:Oh, I'm sorry. I am a little nervous because this is my first flight. Can you show me how to return it back?

旅客:哦,对不起。我有点紧张,因为这是我第一次坐飞机。你能告诉我怎么把座椅靠背调回到直立位置吗?

CA:Oh, I understand. Don't worry, everything will be OK. Just press the button on your armrest, then, look, your seat is back to the upright position.

乘务员:哦,我明白了。别担心,一切都会好的。只需按一下扶手上的按钮,看,您的座位又回到了直立位置。

PAX:Oh, let me try it again. Is that right?

旅客:哦,让我再试一次。是这样吗?

CA:Yes, correct! And please also check that your seat belt is fastened.

乘务员：是的，正确！同时请检查您的安全带是否系好。
PAX：Sorry, Miss. Can you tell me how to fasten the seat belt?
旅客：对不起，小姐。你能告诉我怎么系安全带吗？
CA：All right. Just slip the belt into the buckle and pull tight. Look! Just like this.
乘务员：好的。只需将安全带滑入皮带扣并拉紧即可。看！就这样。
PAX：Oh, I see. Thank you for answering my questions.
旅客：哦，我明白了。谢谢你回答我的问题。
CA：No problem. If you have any other problems, please press the call button, it's there.
乘务员：不用谢。如果您还有其他问题，请按呼叫按钮，它就在那里。
PAX：You are so kind.
旅客：你真是太好了
CA：You are welcome.
乘务员：不客气。

四、广播词

Announcement for Safety Check（安全检查广播）

Ladies and gentlemen,

We will take off soon. Please be seated, fasten your seat belt and make sure that your tray table is closed, your seat back is returned to the upright position. If you are sitting in a window seat, please help us by opening the window shade. We will be dimming the cabin lights. If you want to read, please turn on your reading light. Please do not smoke during the entire fight.

Thank you!

女士们、先生们：

我们的飞机很快就要起飞了，请您配合客舱乘务员的安全检查，系好安全带，收起小桌板，调直座椅靠背，靠窗边的旅客请您协助将遮光板拉开。同时，我们将调暗客舱灯光，如果您需要阅读，请打开阅读灯。本次航班是禁烟航班。

谢谢！

Ladies and gentlemen,

Please note certain electronic devices must not be used on board at any time. These devices include AM/FM radios, televisions and remote control equipment. All other potable electronic devices including laptop computers must not be switched on until 15 minutes after the take-off, or switched to flight mode.

Your cooperation will be much appreciated.

女士们、先生们：

在飞行过程中请您不要使用以下电子设备：调频调幅收音机、便携式电视机、遥控装置等。其他电子设备如手提电脑等，请在飞机起飞后15分钟后使用或切换至飞行模式。

谢谢您的合作！

Ladies and gentlemen,

We are ready for departure. Please fasten your seat belt, open the window shade, put the tray table in place, bring your seat back upright and switch off all the electronic devices, set mobile phone in flight mode. Please do not smoke during the entire flight.

Thank you!

女士们、先生们：

我们的飞机很快就要起飞了，请您系好安全带，收起小桌板，调直椅背，打开遮光板，关闭电子设备的电源，手机请调至飞行模式。本次航班全程禁烟。

谢谢您的合作。

Exercise（练习）

Please fill in the blanks with the appropriate words.

1. May we please have your attention for the safety _____?

2. Pull down the _____ mask! Place it over your face.

3. Ladies and gentlemen, we are entering an area of turbulence. So please fasten your seat _____.

4. Could you tell me how to inflate my life _____?

任务五　起飞前再次确认安全检查

一、常用词汇和表达

security check　安全检查
take-off　n. 起飞
electronic devices　电子设备
switch off　关闭
switch into　切换到
small portable　手机
tray table　小桌板
lithium battery　锂电池
window shade　遮光板
no smoking　禁止吸烟

二、句型练习

1. The plane is about to take off, please return to your seat and fasten your seat belt.
飞机即将起飞，请您回到自己的座位上并系好安全带。

2. To prevent accidental bumps, please fasten your seat belt.

为了防止意外颠簸,请系好您的安全带。

3. Please take good care of your electronic equipment during the flight. Please adjust your phone to flight mode.

飞行过程中请妥善保管您的电子设备,请将手机调至飞行模式。

4. Smoking is prohibited during the flight, please do not smoke in cabins and bathrooms.

飞行全程禁止吸烟,请不要在客舱和卫生间内吸烟。

5. It is forbidden to use lithium batteries to charge mobile phones on the plane.

飞机上禁止使用锂电池给手机充电。

三、对话练习

1

CA:Excuse me,sir.

乘务员:打扰一下,先生。

PAX:What's the matter?

旅客:什么事?

CA:Please return to your seat as soon as possible. Our plane is about to take off.

乘务员:请您尽快回到您的座位上,我们的飞机即将起飞。

PAX:My luggage hasn't been put away yet. I'll put it away first.

旅客:我的行李还没有放好,我要先把它放好。

CA:Can I help you?

乘务员:需要我帮忙吗?

PAX:Could you help me with my luggage? Thank you!

旅客:可以帮我放一下行李吗?谢谢!

CA:No problem.

乘务员:没问题!

2

CA:Excuse me,Miss. I'm sorry.

乘务员:不好意思,小姐。打扰一下。

PAX:What's the matter?

旅客:有什么事情吗?

CA:Please turn off your cell phone. Our plane is about to take off.

乘务员:请将您的手机关机,我们的飞机即将起飞。

PAX:Can I turn it off later? Just for a moment.

旅客:可以等一下再关机吗? 就一会儿。

CA:I'm afraid not. If the phone is not turned off, it will interfere with the plane's signal. You can turn it on until landing.

乘务员:恐怕不行。如果不关机,会干扰飞机的信号。您可以等到降落再开机。

PAX: Oh, I see. I'll turn it off right away.
旅客：哦，原来是这样。我马上关机。
CA: Thank you for your cooperation.
乘务员：感谢您的配合。

四、广播词

1

Ladies and gentlemen,

As our aircraft is taxiing into the runway for take-off. Please fasten your seat belt, pull up the window shade, secure your tray table, bring your seat back upright and unplug your headphones and electronic devices. The large portable electronic devices, such as laptops, should be stowed properly. Please ensure that small portable electronic devices, like cell phones, are switched to the flight mode. You are not permitted to use lithium battery and smoke during the entire flight. Please keep your seat belts fastened in case of sudden turbulence.

Thank you!

女士们、先生们：

现在飞机已经开始滑行，请您系好安全带，打开遮光板，收起小桌板，调直椅背，取下耳机以及连接在座椅电源上的数据连接线，妥善存放笔记本电脑等大型便携式电子设备。手机等小型便携式电子设备请确认已切换至飞行模式。飞行全程禁止吸烟，禁止使用锂电池移动电源给电子设备充电。为防止意外湍流，请您全程系好安全带。

2

Ladies and gentlemen,

We are ready for the take-off. Please make sure your seat belt is securely fastened and portable electronic devices, like mobile phones, have been switched to flight mode. Thank you!

女士们、先生们：

我们的飞机马上就要起飞了，请再次确认您的安全带已扣好系紧，手机等便携式电子设备已调至飞行模式。谢谢！

任务六　行李托运

一、常用词汇和表达

baggage/luggage　n. 行李
overhead compartment　头顶上方的行李架
aisle　n. 过道

exit   n. 出口
galley   n. 厨房
fragile   adj. 易碎的
handcart   n. 手推车
block   v. 堵塞
sight   n. 视野
fit   v. 适合；adj. 适合的
turbulence   n. 湍流
article   n. 物品

二、句型练习

1. The baggage check-in is done here. Please show me your ID card.
行李托运在这里办理，请出示您的证件。
2. Your luggage is already overweight, please pay the extra check-in fee.
您的行李已超重，请支付额外的托运费用。
3. This is the baggage tag. We will affix it to your checked baggage.
这个是行李标签，我们会把它贴到您所托运的行李上。
4. Here is your boarding pass and certificate. Please keep it.
这是您的登机牌和证件，请收好。
5. You need to pick up your checked baggage at the baggage carousel.
您需要在行李转盘处领取托运的行李。

三、对话练习

1

CA：May I have your passport and ticket, please?
乘务员：请出示您的护照和机票好吗？
PAX：Here they are.
旅客：给你。
CA：How many luggage do you have?
乘务员：您有几件行李？
PAX：Two pieces of luggage, one big and one small.
旅客：两件，一大一小。
CA：Anything else?
乘务员：还有别的吗？
PAX：Yes, a handbag.
旅客：是的，一个手提包。
CA：Handbag is free, which can be brought on board with you.
乘务员：手提包是免费的，您可以随身带上飞机。
PAX：I see. Is my luggage overweight?

旅客：我知道。我的行李超重了吗？

CA：Will you please put all your luggage on the scale? It's eight kilos overweight the baggage allowance, which will be charged for excess luggage fee.

乘务员：请您把行李过一下磅好吗？超了8千克，要付超重费。

PAX：How much should I pay?

旅客：我应该付多少钱？

CA：Eighty dollars. And you can pay it here.

乘务员：80美元，您可以在这里付款。

PAX：OK. Here you are.

旅客：好的，给你。

CA：These are the luggage labels. Please fasten them on your luggage and here is your passport, ticket and boarding pass. Take care of them.

乘务员：这些是行李标签，请把它们绑紧在您的行李上。这是您的护照、机票和登机牌，请拿好。

PAX：Thank you!

旅客：谢谢！

2

PAX：Good morning, Miss. Can I check in for SQ821?

旅客：早上好，女士。我能办理航班号是SQ821的登机手续吗？

CA：Yes. May I have your passport and ticket, please?

乘务员：可以，请出示您的机票和护照好吗？

PAX：Here you are.

旅客：给你。

CA：Please put your two pieces of baggage on the conveyor belt one by one.

乘务员：请把您的两件行李依次放在传送带上。

PAX：OK. I'll go to Hong Kong first, and then take a connecting flight to Bangkok. What else should I do?

旅客：好的，我将先去香港转机，然后再到曼谷，我还要做些什么吗？

CA：You mean your destination is Bangkok, right? Then you can check in your baggage all the way through to Bangkok.

乘务员：您的意思是您的目的地是曼谷，是吧？那么您可以直接托运行李至曼谷。

PAX：Can I? I don't know before.

旅客：可以吗？以前我都不知道。

CA：Yes, of course you can. I will label your baggage as the interlined one. The baggage handler will take care of them.

乘务员：是的，当然可以。我会在您的行李上贴上中转标签，这样搬运工就会小心处理了。

PAX：Thanks! You just save me a lot of trouble.

旅客：谢谢！您真帮了我一个大忙。

四、广播词

Ladies and gentlemen,

Good morning. If there are passengers who need to check their baggage, please have your ID card and boarding pass and go to the counter to handle it. Thank you!

女士们、先生们：

早上好。有需要托运行李的旅客，请您拿好您的身份证件和登机牌，到柜台处办理，谢谢！

Exercise（练习）

1. Please fill in the blanks with the appropriate words.

（1）May we please have your attention for the safety _____?

（2）Pull down the _____ mask! Place it over your face.

（3）Ladies and gentlemen, we are entering an area of turbulence. So please fasten your seat _____.

（4）Could you tell me how to inflate my life _____?

2. Please fill in the blanks with the exact words or phrases according to the first letter.

Emergency and Survival Equipment

As we all know, there is e _____ and survival equipment on board all a _____. The emergency equipment includes emergency lights, flashlights, and megaphone. The survival equipment c _____ of life v _____, slide rafts, escape slides, and escape ropes, descent d _____ and survival kit.

All exits are e _____ with exit signs above and adjacent to the exits. In addition, lighted signs are displayed above the a _____ or on partitions to indicate the location of emergency e _____. In the cabin, lighted floor path markings l _____ you towards the exits. This emergency lighting system will come on a _____ in the event of electrical power failure, or it can be switched on m _____ via cockpit or cabin switches.

项目小结

起飞前的广播主要包括登机广播、安全演示、安全检查等内容，需要乘务员对旅客进行广播，以便更好地帮助与指引旅客登机。不同内容的广播还要运用不同的语气。例如，登机广播的主要目的是问候旅客，与旅客确认所乘航班的承运航空公司及相关信息，并告知旅客行李摆放的位置，请旅客快速入座。朗读这一广播稿时应语气亲切，涉及航空公司名称、航线、机型、行李摆放位置以及要求旅客保持通道和出口畅通等词语应重读。再如广播禁用电子设备的目的是让旅客了解飞行各个阶段使用电子设备的限制和规定，并提醒旅客在飞机起飞前关闭相应电子设备。在朗读时应语气坚定，提及电子设备时，应发音清晰且重读。

项目训练

1. 在航班起飞前,你发现一名旅客没有将行李放在头顶行李架或者座椅下方。假如你是乘务员,应如何对旅客进行客舱安全广播?

2. 根据航班起飞前客舱内可能发生的各种状况,各小组拟写广播词,模仿乘务员和不同旅客。每个小组在模拟时,其他小组要认真观看,并做好记录。然后根据民航广播播音用语的基本要求进行自我评价,并与其他小组进行互评。

项 目	考核要点	完成情况	评定等级
客舱广播	播报及时		
	播报语气适当		
	广播词格式符合规范		
	广播词表达准确		
	语音音量适中		
	语调生动		
综合评定等级			

项目四　飞行中服务广播

项目目标

知识目标

了解飞行中广播词的内涵和用途；

掌握飞行中广播词的核心要素；

了解如何导入飞行中广播词。

能力目标

通过对飞行中常见广播词理论知识的学习，端正服务态度，培养民航服务意识，做好对客服务的心理准备、思想准备和行为准备。

素质目标

掌握飞行中广播词的语言规范要求，提高自身文化修养。

知识框架

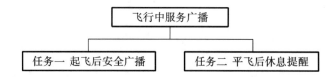

任务一　起飞后安全广播

一、常用词汇和表达

block　v. 阻碍

emergency exit　紧急出口

galley　n. 厨房

litter　n. 垃圾

fragile item　易碎品

turbulence   n. 湍流

dispose   v. 处理

preparation   n. 预备, 准备

departure   n. 离开, 出发

prohibit   v. 阻止, 禁止

flight mode   飞行模式

cash   n. 现款, 现金

valuable items   贵重物品

electronic   adj. 电子的

device   n. 装置

restriction   n. 限制

cellular phone   手机

remote   adj. 远程的, 遥远的

laptop computer   n. 笔记本电脑

switch on/off   打开/关闭

二、句型练习

1. Our plane has taken off. Please make sure your seat belt is securely fastened.

我们的飞机已经起飞了, 请确认您的安全带已扣好系紧。

2. Please ensure that small portable electronic devices, like cell phones, are switched to the flight mode.

请将手机等小型便携电子设备确认切换至飞行模式。

3. Please keep your seat belt fastened in case of sudden turbulence.

为防止意外湍流, 请您全程系好安全带。

4. We have now reached the cruising altitude. To prevent injury from turbulence, please keep your seat belt fastened during the entire flight.

飞机已到达安全高度, 为了防止湍流造成伤害, 请您全程系好安全带。

5. For further information, please refer to the safety instruction in the seat pocket in front of you.

《安全须知》在您前排座椅背后的口袋里, 请您在起飞前仔细阅读。

6. For you safety, please return to your seat and keep your seat belt fastened.

为了您的安全, 请您在座位上坐好并系好安全带。

7. The plane has taken off. For your safety, please remain seated with your seat belt fastened until the seat belt sign goes off.

飞机已经起飞。请您在座位上坐好, 系好安全带, 直到安全带指示灯熄灭。

三、对话练习

1

CA:Excuse me, sir.

乘务员:打扰了,先生。

PAX:Yes?

旅客:怎么了?

CA:You can't put your luggage on your lap.

乘务员:您不能把行李放在腿上。

PAX:Why? It's not in anyone's way.

旅客:为什么? 这不会妨碍任何人。

CA:Here's the thing, sir. If you put the luggage on your leg, the luggage may hurt people when the plane is hit.

乘务员:是这样的,先生。如果将行李放在腿上,飞机受到冲击时,行李可能会伤到人。

PAX:So where could I put it?

旅客:我该把它放在哪?

CA:You can put your luggage in the overhead compartment or under the seat.

乘务员:您可以把行李放在头顶行李架或者座椅下方。

PAX:All right.

旅客:好的。

2

PAX:Excuse me, Miss. May I put my luggage here?

旅客:打扰一下,小姐。我可以把行李放到这里吗?

CA:I'm afraid not. This is the emergency exit position. No luggage is allowed.

乘务员:恐怕不可以。这里是紧急出口位置,是不允许放任何行李的。

PAX:But my baggage is too big to go into the overhead compartment or under my seat.

旅客:但是我的行李太大了,放不进行李架或座位下面。

CA:Well, if you don't mind, I'll keep it safe somewhere else.

乘务员:嗯,如果您不介意的话,我会把它保管到别处的。

PAX:Thank you.

旅客:谢谢!

3

CA:Excuse me, sir. We have now reached the cruising altitude. To prevent injury from turbulence, please keep your seat belt fastened during the entire flight.

乘务员:打扰一下,先生。我们现在已经到达巡航高度。为了防止湍流造成的伤害,请在整个飞行过程中系好安全带。

PAX:OK, I will do it right away.

旅客:好的,我马上就做。

CA:Sorry, sir, please set your mobile phone to flight mode for safety.

乘务员：对不起，先生，为了安全起见，请将您的手机设置为飞行模式。
PAX：Alright.
旅客：好的。
CA：Thank you for your cooperation.
乘务员：谢谢您的合作。

四、广播词

1 Safety Announcement After Take-off 起飞后安全广播

Ladies and gentlemen,
May I have your attention please?
We are climbing now and we may encounter some turbulence. For your safety, please remain seated and fasten your seat belt.
Thank you!

女士们、先生们：
我们的飞机正在上升高度，可能会遇到湍流。为了您的安全，请您在座位上坐好，并系好安全带。
谢谢！

2 Safety Announcement During Fly Evenly 平飞广播

Ladies and gentlemen,
Our plane has left _____ to _____. Along this route, the provinces we fly through are _____, The main cities passed by are _____, we will also fly over _____.
During this journey, we prepared _____ meals for you. We'll broadcast when we serve.

女士们、先生们：
我们的飞机已经离开_____前往_____，沿这条航线，我们经过的省份有_____，经过的主要城市有_____，我们还将飞越_____。
在这段旅途中，我们为您准备了_____餐。供餐时我们将广播通知您。

3 Announcement for Serving Meals 供餐广播

Ladies and Gentlemen,
We are pleased to begin our meal services. Flight attendants will be moving through the cabin serving meals and beverages soon. For the convenience of the passenger siting behind you, please adjust your seat back to its upright and locked position during the meal service.
If you need any assistance, please contact us.

女士们、先生们：
我们将为您提供餐食及各种饮料。在用餐期间，请您调直座椅靠背，以方便后排的旅客。如需要帮助,请随时联系我们。

谢谢!

4　Safety Announcement 安全广播

Ladies and gentlemen,

We have now reached the cruising altitude. To prevent injury from turbulence, please keep your seat belt fastened during the entire flight.

Thank you.

女士们、先生们:

飞机已经到达安全高度,为了防止湍流造成的伤害,请您全程系好安全带。

谢谢。

五、补充阅读

飞行期间的注意事项

1. 请一定要认真看乘务员示范的相关动作,比如,如何使用氧气面罩,等等。在您座位前方,有说明如何使用救生工具,以及如何在紧急情况下逃生的图片。无论在飞行途中遇到任何情况,请不要慌张,安抚好您的家人和小孩。我们的乘务员和安全员都接受过专门的培训,有足够的经验去协调和帮助旅客,所以一定要听从他们的指挥,切勿乱成一团。

We must carefully watch the relevant actions demonstrated by the flight attendants, such as how to wear and use oxygen masks and so on. In front of your seat, there are pictures showing how to use life-saving tools and how to escape in an emergency. No matter what happens during the flight, don't panic and comfort your family and children. Our flight attendants and safety officers have received special training and have enough experience to coordinate and help passengers, so we must obey their instructions and do not mess up.

2. 飞行全程务必系好安全带,还要知道如何快速解开安全带。如果坐在紧急出口旁边,首先要清楚怎样打开紧急出口。如果你在紧急情况下不知道操作方法,不仅自己的安全会受到威胁,还会给别人带来危险。紧急出口非常沉,你得有足够的力气才能打开它。

Be sure to fasten your seat belt during the whole flight. And know how to unfasten your seat belt quickly. If you're sitting next to an emergency exit, figure out how to open it first. If you don't know how to operate in an emergency, not only your own safety will be threatened, but also others will be in danger. The emergency exit is very heavy. You have to have enough strength to open it.

Exercise(练习)

1. Please fill in the blanks with the appropriate words.

(1) We have just experienced some serious _____ there.

(2) For the _____ of your property.

(3) May I have your _____, please?

(4) The captain has turned on the _____ seat belt sign.

2. Please fill in the blanks with the exact words or phrases according to the first letter.

In-flight Service

Ladies and gentlemen,

The captain has turned off the f_____ seat belt sign, and you may now move around the c_____. However we always r_____ to keep your seat belt fastened while you are seated.

In a few m_____, the fight attendants will be passing around the cabin to offer you hot or cold drinks, as well as breakfast/dinner/supper/a light meal/a snack. Alcoholic drinks are also a_____ at a nominal charge/with our compliments. (On long fights with in-flight e_____. Also, we will be showing you our video presentation.) Now, sit back, relax, and e_____ the fight. Thank you.

任务二　平飞后休息提醒

一、常用词汇和表达

button　n. 按钮
recline　v. 斜倚
press　v. 按，压
armrest　n. 扶手
pillow　n. 枕头
slippers　n. 拖鞋
blanket　n. 毯子
air conditioner　n. 空调
reading light　阅读灯
ear plugs　耳塞
headset　n. 耳机
eye mask　眼罩
lean back　向后倾
set a channel　设置频道
crew call button　机组呼叫按钮
amenity kit/overnight kit　便利设施/过夜设施

二、句型练习

1. What can I do for you?
我能为您提供什么样的帮助？

2. May I insist you on adjusting the seat?

我可以要求您调整一下座位吗?

3. The lavatory is at the back/at the front.

厕所在后面/前面.

4. Press this button and lean back.

按这个按钮向后靠。

5. Here is the toy for your child.

这是给您孩子的玩具。

6. It's quite cold. Would you like a cup of hot tea?

真是太冷了。您想喝杯热茶吗?

7. Air travel is the safest means of modern travel.

航空旅行是现代旅行最安全的方式。

8. Sir, may I lower the window shade for you?

先生,我可以帮您把遮光帘放下吗?

9. Would you like an extra pillow and blanket?

您需要额外的枕头和毯子吗?

10. We are pleased to answer any question at any time.

我们乐意随时回答任何问题。

11. We will be right here with you anytime you press the call button.

只要您按呼叫按钮,我们就会过来。

12. Would you like to put on slippers? You will be more comfortable with it.

您想穿拖鞋吗? 您会觉得更舒服。

三、对话练习

CA:Hello, sir, I saw you turn on the yellow light, what can I do for you?

乘务员:您好,先生,我看您打开了求助黄灯,需要什么帮助?

PAX:One of the headsets does not work. Please change it for me.

旅客:这副耳机有一边没有声音。请换一副。

CA:Sure, wait a moment, please. (A moment later) Here it is. How does this one work?

乘务员:好的,请稍等。给您。现在这副怎样呢?

PAX:I can not hear it clearly. The volume is too low, I am afraid.

旅客:我听得不是很清楚。声音有点小。

CA:Well, the controls are located on top of your seat armrest. If you want to be louder, you could press that button with upside arrow.

乘务员:选择按钮在您的座椅扶手上方。如果您想调大声点,可以按那个带向上箭头的按钮。

PAX:This one? It does work. It's better now. Thank you!

旅客:是这个按钮吗？挺管用的。现在好多了,谢谢你!

CA:You are welcome. We have plenty of choices on the flight, ranging from pop music to opera. You may press that one to choose your favorite.

乘务员:不客气。本次航班我们提供多种选择,从流行音乐到戏剧。您可以按那个按钮来选择您喜欢的音乐。

四、广播词

Night Flight(夜航广播)

1

Ladies and gentlemen,

To ensure a good rest for every passenger, we will turn off the video system and dim the cabin lights. Please fasten your seat belt. If there is any thing we can do for you, please let us know.

Thank you!

女士们、先生们:

为了使您有一个舒适的休息环境,我们将关闭客舱音乐,调暗客舱灯光。休息时请您系好安全带。如果您需要帮助,请随时告知我们。

谢谢!

2

Good evening, ladies and gentlemen,

To ensure a good rest for you, we will be dimming the cabin light. If you wish to read, please turn the reading light on.

Your safety is our primary concern, we strongly recommend you keep your seat belt fastened throughout the flight.

Your cooperation in keeping the cabin quiet will be appreciated. If you need any assistance, please press the call button.

Thank you!

女士们、先生们,晚上好!

为了让您休息好,我们将调暗机舱灯光。如果您想阅读,请打开阅读灯。

您的安全是我们最关心的问题,我们强烈建议您在整个飞行过程中系好安全带。

感谢您保持机舱安静。如果您需要帮助,请按呼叫按钮。

谢谢!

Cabin Installations(介绍机舱设施广播)

Good morning/afternoon/evening, ladies and gentlemen,

Our aircraft for today's flight is Boeing.

Your seat back can be adjusted by pressing the button on your armrest. The reading light, call button and air vents are located above your head.

The lavatory for first class passengers is in the front of the aircraft and those in the rear of the aircraft are for passengers in main cabin. (Lavatories in the front and rear of the cabin are all available.)

If there is anything we can do for you, please let us know.

Thank you!

女士们、先生们,早上/下午/晚上好!

此次航班的飞机是波音公司的。

按扶手上的按钮可以调节座椅靠背。阅读灯、呼叫按钮和通风口位于您头顶上方。

头等舱旅客的厕所在飞机的前部,而飞机后部的厕所供主客舱的旅客使用。(客舱的前部和后部都有厕所。)

如果您需要帮助,请及时告知我们。

谢谢!

以下节日需要广播节日祝福:

女士们、先生们,早上/下午/晚上好!

今天是_____节日,在此祝您节日快乐!

Good morning/afternoon/evening, ladies and gentlemen,

Today is..., we wish you a happy holiday.

元旦 New Year's Day

除夕 New Year's Eve

春节 Spring Festival/Chinese New Year

元宵节 Lantern Festival

五一国际劳动节 International Worker's Day

端午节 Dragon Boat Festival

中秋节 Mid-Autumn Day

国庆节 National Day

感恩节 Thanksgiving Day

圣诞节 Christmas; Merry Christmas

Exercise(练习)

1. Please fill in the blanks with the appropriate words.

(1) To ensure you rest well in the long _____.

(2) Please keep your seat belt fastened and take care of your _____ items at all times.

(3) If you need any _____, please contact us.

(4) Just press the _____ on the armrest.

2. Please fill in the blanks with the exact words or phrases according to the first letter.

Remind to Fasten the Seat Belt

Time: After the first meal service

Notice: Economy cabin only.

Ladies and gentlemen,

We will dim the c_____ light. In case of sudden t_____, please fasten your seat belt when seated, and make sure it is visible at all times, so that cabin crew have no need d_____ you. We will be by your side anytime you need anything from us.

Thank you.

Trip Plan

Ladies and gentlemen,

Breakfast/lunch/dinner/refreshment is about to be offered after _____ hours _____ minutes prior to landing.

(And the duty free sales will begin after the meal)

Please keep your seat belt fastened when seated in case of s_____ turbulence. Once again, all m_____ phones need to be t_____ off during the e_____ flight. (While using your personal l_____, please make sure the WiFi f_____ has been switched off.) We will be by your side anytime you need anything from us. We wish you a p_____ trip.

项目小结

在飞行过程中,通过相应的客舱广播可以创设良好的服务氛围,给广大旅客带来轻松、愉悦、舒适之感,使广大旅客能够通过客舱广播对空中乘务人员的工作内容有一个更清晰明确的认识,确保广大旅客能够积极配合空中乘务人员的各项工作。空中乘务人员通过客舱广播,能够有效提升同旅客之间的沟通效果,构建一个良性服务系统,使空中服务协调、统一。

项目训练

1. 在航班起飞后,需要对旅客进行安全广播和提醒。根据这个情境,每个小组拟写一份广播词并在课上进行播报展示。

项目	考核要点	完成情况	评定等级
客舱广播	播报及时		
	播报语气适当		
	广播词格式符合规范		
	广播词表达准确		
	语音音量适中		
	语调生动		
综合评定等级			

2. 小组合作,自设情景(起飞后的安全提醒)并合理运用客舱广播用语组织对话,拍成视频,上传至班级QQ群中。

项目五　着陆后服务广播

项目目标

- **知识目标**

  了解飞机着陆后广播词的内涵和用途；

  掌握飞机着陆后广播词的核心要素；

  了解如何导入着陆后广播词。

- **能力目标**

  通过对飞机着陆后常见广播词理论知识的学习，端正服务态度，培养民航服务意识，做好对客服务的心理准备、思想准备和行为准备。

- **素质目标**

  掌握着陆后广播词的语言规范要求，提高自身文化修养。

知识框架

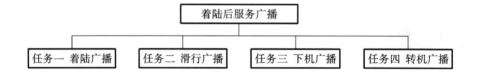

任务一　着陆广播

一、常用词汇和表达

descend　v. 下降

landing　n. 着陆

terminate　v. 结束，使终结

unfasten　v. 松开，解开

disembark　v. 登陆，上岸，下飞机

apron n. 停机坪
PAX count 清点旅客人数
ground temperature 地面温度
Fasten the Seat Belt Sign 系好安全带标志
landing gear 起落架
cabin safety announcement 客舱安全广播
cruising level 巡航高度
International Date Line 国际日期变更线
degree Celsius 摄氏温度
degree Fahrenheit 华氏温度

二、句型练习

1. The time difference between Beijing and Madrid is 6 hours. We are expected to arrive at 3:25 p.m. local time on September 25.

北京与马德里的时差为6小时,我们预计在当地时间9月25日下午3点25分到达。

2. If you are not able to find a satisfactory item on this flight, you can make a reservation by filling in the reservation form, and we will try our best to meet your requirements on the next leg of the flight you booked.

如果您在本次航班中未能选到满意的商品,您可以通过填写预订单预订所需商品,我们会在您预订的下一段航班中尽量满足您的需求。

3. For your safety, please fasten your seat belt the whole time.

为了您的安全,请全程系好安全带。

4. The plane has started to descend. Please adjust your seat back, put down your armrests, put your tray table and pedals back up, fasten your seat belt, and open the window shade.

飞机已经开始下降。请您调直座椅靠背,放下座椅扶手,收起小桌板和脚踏板,系好安全带,打开遮光板。

5. Our crew would like to express our most sincere thanks to you for your support and assistance during the journey.

对您在旅途中给予我们的支持和帮助,全体机组人员向您表示最诚挚的谢意。

6. The onboard lavatories will not be used.

机上洗手间将停止使用。

7. Thank you for your understanding.

谢谢您的理解。

8. Thank you for your cooperation.

谢谢您的合作。

三、对话练习

CA:Would you like to have a look at our duty-free items,sir?

乘务员:先生,您想看看我们的免税商品吗?

PAX:Yes. I am thinking about buying something for my father. He doesn't drink or smoke. What could you recommend?

旅客:是的,我在考虑给我父亲买点东西。他既不喝酒也不抽烟。你能推荐一下吗?

CA:What about a silk tie or handkerchief.

乘务员:丝绸领带或手帕怎么样?

PAX:Where are they made?

旅客:它们是在哪里生产的?

CA:They are made in Hangzhou,a city famous for its silk production in China.

乘务员:它们是杭州生产的,杭州以丝绸生产而闻名。

PAX:Good idea! How much are they together?

旅客:好主意!它们一共多少钱?

CA:40 US dollars.

乘务员:40美元。

PAX:Can you give me a discount?

旅客:可以给我一个折扣吗?

CA:Sorry,I can't. All items on board are sold at marked price.

乘务员:不好意思,我不能。机上的所有物品都以标价出售。

PAX:All right. I'll take them. Can I pay by credit cards?

旅客:好的。我可以用信用卡支付吗?

CA:Yes,of course. We have a card reader on board.

乘务员:当然可以。飞机上有一个读卡器。

PAX:What kind of cards do you accept?

旅客:你接受什么样的卡?

CA:Most major credit cards are accepted for your purchase,such as Master Card, Visa Card and American Express.

乘务员:大多数信用卡都可以用来购买,例如万事达卡、Visa卡和美国运通卡。

四、广播词

机组通知起落架放下后

Ladies and gentlemen,

We are ready for landing,please double-check your seat belt is securely fastened and all electronic devices are switched off.

Thank you.

女士们、先生们:

飞机即将着陆,请再次确认安全带已经系好,所有电子设备已关闭。谢谢!

机组通知飞机落地后

Ladies and gentlemen,

Our plane has landed at _____ Airport. The local time is _____. The temperature outside is _____ degrees Celsius, (_____ degrees Fahrenheit). The plane is taxiing. For your safety, please stay in your seat for the time being. When the aircraft stops completely and the Fasten Seat Belt sign is turned off, please detach the seat belt, take all your carry-on items and disembark/take all your carry-on items and passport to complete the entry formalities in the terminal. Please be cautious when retrieving items from the overhead compartment. Your checked baggage may be claimed in the baggage claim area. The transit passengers please go to the connection flight counter in the waiting hall to complete the procedures.

It is raining/snowing outside, please be careful while getting out of the plane.

女士们、先生们：

我们已抵达_____机场。当地时间是_____。机舱外温度_____摄氏度（_____华氏度）。

飞机正在滑行。为了您的安全，请您在座位上耐心等候。等飞机完全停好、安全带指示灯熄灭后再解开安全带，带好您的随身物品下飞机/带好您的随身物品和护照到航站楼办理入境手续。从行李架取行李时，请注意安全，您的托运行李请到候机楼行李提取处领取，需要转机的旅客请到转机台办理手续。

外面正在下雨/雪，下飞机时请注意地面路滑。

五、补充阅读

What Do the Cabin Attendants Do before Landing?

The cabin attendants have so many tasks to perform in the last minutes before landing. Many of these tasks might be called cleaning-up chores. For example, they return all equipments to the appropriate storage areas. They also clean galleys and the lavatory areas and turn off all switches in the galleys. They have to gather up pillows, blankets and magazines.

On a final cabin check. The cabin attendants will check to see that all seat belts are fastened and seat backs are in the upright position. The seat tables must be stowed, and passengers are cautioned against smoking. If it is an international flight, they also check that all passengers and crew members have filled in all necessary documents.

There are also several announcements to be made before arrival. The first notifies the passengers that the flight will be landing in a few minutes. At the same time, local time and weather conditions are announced. If the plane is making a transit stop—that is, if it will continue on to another destination after the stop—the length of time the plane staying on the ground is also announced. The passengers are also advised to take their personal effects with them and to have their travel documents ready.

Announcements are also made when the seat belt and non-smoking signs are turned on. If they are landing at an airport where local health regulations require that the plane be sprayed against insects, there will also be a spray announcement so that the passengers will know what is happening.

空乘人员在着陆前做什么？

在飞机着陆前的最后几分钟,乘务员有很多工作要做。这些工作中有许多被称为"清扫杂务"。例如,他们将所有设备放回到正确的存储区域。他们还清洁厨房和洗手间,并关闭厨房的所有开关。他们还要收拾枕头、毯子和杂志。

最后检查一下机舱。乘务员将检查所有的安全带是否系好,座椅靠背是否处于直立状态。座椅上的小桌板必须收好,并告诫旅客不要吸烟。如果是国际航班,他们还会检查所有旅客和机组人员是否填写了所有必要的文件。

在到达之前还有几件事要广播。第一是通知旅客飞机将在几分钟后着陆,同时告知当地时间和天气情况。如果飞机是过境停留,即过境后继续飞往另一个目的地,飞机在地面停留的时间也要被告知。此外,旅客应随身携带个人物品,并准备好旅行证件。

当安全带和禁止吸烟指示灯亮起时,也要广播。如果飞机降落在当地卫生法规要求喷洒防虫剂的机场,也会发布喷洒通告,让旅客知道发生了什么。

一、常用词汇和表达

taxiing　滑行
go off　熄灭
open the overhead compartment　打开头顶上方的行李架
fall out　滑落
prohibit　v. 禁止
upright position　垂直位置
buckle　n. 搭扣,扣环
turn off　关闭
navigation　n. 航行
call button　呼叫按钮

二、句型练习

Would you please return your seat back to the upright position?
请您将您的座椅靠背调回到直立位置好吗?

You have to wait until we come to a complete stop.

您必须等我们完全停下来。

Thank you for helping me.

感谢您帮助我。

Thank you for your cooperation.

谢谢您的合作。

If you have any other problems, please press the call button.

如果您有其他问题, 请按呼叫按钮。

三、对话练习

1

CA:Excuse me, sir. Please return to your seat.

乘务员:不好意思,先生,请您回到座位上。

PAX:But I need to go to the bathroom now. I've been waiting for a long time.

旅客:但是我现在需要上厕所。我已经等了很久了。

CA:I'm sorry, sir. The plane is taxiing now. Please return to your seat and fasten your seat belt.

乘务员:对不起,先生。飞机现在正在滑行。请您回到座位并系好安全带。

PAX:Please, I'll be out soon.

旅客:拜托,我很快就出来。

CA:Please wait a little longer, our plane will finish taxiing soon. For your own safety, please sit down first.

乘务员:麻烦您再等一会,我们的飞机马上结束滑行。为了您的安全,请您还是先坐好。

PAX:All right, I'll wait a little longer.

旅客:好吧,我再等一会儿。

CA:Thank you for your understanding.

乘务员:感谢您的理解。

2

CA:Excuse me, Miss. Please don't open the overhead compartment now.

乘务员:不好意思,小姐。现在请不要打开头顶行李架。

PAX:I need to take my luggage, which is very important to me.

旅客:我需要拿一下我的行李,这对我来说很重要。

CA:The plane is taxiing. For your safety, please don't open the overhead luggage compartment. Wait for the plane to stop and then open it.

乘务员:飞机正在滑行,为了您的安全,请不要打开头顶行李架。等飞机停稳后再打开。

PAX:Okay. How long will it take for the plane to stop?

旅客:好吧。飞机大概还有多久才能停稳?

CA:Almost done. Please wait patiently.

乘务员:马上就好。请您耐心等待。

PAX:OK.

旅客:好的。

CA:Thank you for your cooperation.

乘务员:感谢您的配合。

四、广播词

Ladies and gentlemen,

The aircraft is taxiing now. For your safety, please remain seated with your seat belt fastened until the seat belt sign goes off. Please be careful when opening the overhead compartment, as items inside may fall out. Kindly take all your belongings with you when leaving the aircraft.

It's been our pleasure to serve you on this flight. Thank you for taking our flight. We look forward to seeing you again in the near future.

Thank you.

女士们、先生们:

飞机正在滑行,请您在座位上坐好,系好安全带,直到安全带指示灯熄灭。请您小心打开行李架取行李,以免行李滑落。下机时,请您带齐所有的行李物品。我们很高兴为您服务,感谢您选乘本次航班。期待与您再次相会。

谢谢。

五、补充阅读

1 Slide Reason(滑行原因)

The reason why the aircraft taxis after landing is that its power system is relatively developed and will continue to work during the descent. Therefore, taxiing needs to be used to play a buffer role, so as to stop at the specified parking port.

飞机降落后之所以要滑行,是因为它的动力系统比较发达,下降时依旧会继续工作,所以需要滑行起到缓冲作用,从而停靠到规定的停机口。

2 Points to Note for Taxiing(滑行注意事项)

Aircraft taxiing is the important stage in the whole flight process. In order to ensure passengers' safety and smooth flight, we should do "three must and three don't". "Three must" are, to fasten the seat belt, to put down the tray table, to adjust the seat to the normal position; the "three don't" are, don't leave your seat, don't walk back and forth, and don't open the overhead compartment for your luggage.

飞机滑行是整个飞行过程中的重要阶段。为保证旅客安全,顺利完成乘机旅行,要做到"三要、三不要"。"三要"是要系好安全带,要收起小桌板,要把座椅调整到正常位置;"三不要"是不要离开座位,不要来回走动,不要打开行李架取行李。

任务三　下机广播

一、常用词汇和表达

baggage carousel　行李转盘
service counter　服务柜台
baggage claim　行李领取处
exit　n. 出口
transfer　n. 中转
personal belongings　随身物品
slip　v. 滑落
assistance　n. 帮助
cabin door　舱门
gallery bridge　廊桥

二、句型练习

For your safety, please keep your seat belt fastened.
为了您的安全，请保持安全带系好。
Please do not use your cell phone until the cabin door is open.
客舱门打开之前请不要使用手机。
Take special care not to let your luggage slip.
请特别留意，以免行李滑落。
Before disembarking, please check again around your seat to make sure you have all your personal belongings with you.
下机前，请再次检查座椅周围，确认您已携带好所有随身物品。
Thank you for choosing to fly with us.
感谢您选择我们的航班。
Wish you all the best.
祝您一切顺利。
Looking forward to serving you again.
期待再次为您服务。
Our crew would like to express our most sincere thanks to you for your support and assistance during the journey.
对您在旅途中给予我们的支持和帮助，我们全体机组人员表示最诚挚的谢意。

三、对话练习

1

CA:Excuse me,Miss.

乘务员:不好意思,小姐。

PAX:Yes,Miss?

旅客:什么事,小姐?

CA:Why don't you sit down and fasten your seat belt?

乘务员:您为什么不坐下来系好安全带呢?

PAX:I want to go to the lavatory.

旅客:我想去厕所。

CA:I'm sorry,you can't use the lavatory now. The plane is descending and is going to land in a few minutes.

乘务员:抱歉,您现在不能去厕所了。飞机正在下降,几分钟后即将着陆。

PAX:All right.

旅客:好的。

CA:Let me help you fasten the seat belt.

乘务员:让我帮您系好安全带。

2

PAX:Excuse me,Miss. I've lost track completely. What time and what day is it?

旅客:不好意思,小姐。我完全迷糊了。现在是几号几点啊?

CA:It's Thursday,May 21 and 3:20 in the afternoon,Beijing local time.

乘务员:北京时间5月21日星期四下午3点20分。

PAX:Well,my watch is showing Wednesday,May 20 and 3:20 in the morning.

旅客:我的表显示5月20日星期三,凌晨3点20分。

CA:Yes,New York is 12 hours behind of Beijing but one day behind,because we cross the International Date Line.

乘务员:是的,纽约比北京晚了12个小时,但是晚了一天,因为我们越过了国际日期变更线。

PAX:That sounds very complicated,but I'll put it 12 hours backward for Beijing. May I ask another question?

旅客:这听起来很复杂,我要把它放在晚于北京的12个小时里。我可以再问一个问题吗?

CA:Sure,of course.

乘务员:当然可以。

PAX:What was the weather like in New York when I arrived?

旅客:我到纽约的时候,纽约的天气怎么样?

CA:According to the weather report,it was sunny there.

乘务员:根据天气预报,那里阳光明媚。

PAX:That will be wonderful. Thank you, Miss.
旅客:那就太好了。谢谢你,小姐。
CA:You're welcome, Madam.
乘务员:不客气,女士。

四、广播词

After cabin door opened(舱门打开后)

Ladies and gentlemen,

We are broadcasting the carousel information. You may collect your checked baggage at carousel Number _____. To any customer who has the connecting flight, please go to your nearest transfer service counter, you may also contact the ground staff for further assistance.

(AS it is raining/snowing outside, please prepare your umbrella or raincoat for disembark, and mind your steps.) Thank you!

女士们、先生们:

现在为您播报本次航班托运行李的信息。下机后,请到_____号行李转盘提取您的托运行李。如您需要转机,可前往就近的中转服务柜台或向地面工作人员寻求帮助。

(机外正在下雨/下雪,请您准备好雨伞或雨衣。地面湿滑,请您当心脚下。)

谢谢!

任务四 转机广播

一、常用词汇和表达

upgrading   v. 升舱
waiting lounge   候机厅
transit counter   中转服务柜台
connecting flight boarding pass   转机登机牌
transit bus   摆渡车
according to customs regulations   根据海关规定

二、句型练习

Please go to the corresponding counter when you arrive at the terminal building.
请您在到达候机楼后前往相应的柜台办理。

You can check in directly, so you don't have to pick up your checked luggage.

直接办理转机手续,您可以不用提取托运行李。

Go to the transfer counter to check in your luggage.

前往中转服务柜台办理行李再托运。

三、对话练习

PAX:I feel annoyed about landing at the alternate airport! I am going to make a complaint to your airlines authority.

旅客:我对降落在备降机场而感到恼火!我要向你们航空公司投诉。

CA:We are awfully sorry for the inconvenience caused by the severe weather conditions over Beijing Capital International Airport. However, we made the decision to land at the alternate airport for the safety of all passengers.

乘务员:我们对北京首都国际机场的恶劣天气给您带来的不便深表歉意。不过,为了所有旅客的安全,我们决定在备降机场降落。

PAX:Where shall we stay? Shall we spend the night in the waiting lounge?

旅客:我们住在哪里?我们要在候机厅过夜吗?

CA:Of course not. We have made arrangement for the overnight accommodations in the airport hotel. Don't worry about it.

乘务员:当然不是。我们已经安排住在机场酒店。不用担心。

PAX:Who will pay for it?

旅客:谁来付钱?

CA:It is on our treat.

乘务员:我们付钱。

PAX:When will we depart tomorrow?

旅客:我们明天什么时候出发?

CA:I don't know the exact re-take-off time for sure now. We will keep you informed of the updated information.

乘务员:我现在还不知道确切的起飞时间,我们会随时通知您。

PAX:I feel much more comforted now. Thank you for your patience, Miss.

旅客:我现在感觉舒服多了。谢谢你的耐心,小姐。

CA:Your understanding would be greatly appreciated. Have a good rest and see you tomorrow.

乘务员:非常感谢您的理解,好好休息,再见。

四、广播词

Ladies and gentlemen,

We are broadcasting transit information.

Passengers for Airport _____, please collect your baggage at baggage carousel

_____. If you are transiting to _____, your flight will be boarding at Gate _____. The estimated time of departure is _____.

Please pay attention to the flight information board at the airport to see if there are any change in the Boarding Gate of your next flight. Thank you!

女士们、先生们：

现在为您播报转机信息。

到达_____机场的旅客，下机后您可以在_____号行李转盘提取您的行李。

如您在本站转机前往_____，您乘坐的航班的登机口在_____号，预计起飞时间为_____。

为确保顺利成行，建议您关注机场实时信息，看您下一段航班的登机口是否有变化。谢谢！

Transit in Australia

Time：25 minutes before landing

Ladies and gentlemen，

Passengers taking Qantas Airways Flights QF399 or below，can go through transit procedures directly，by following the directions in the waiting hall. You do not have to collect your checked baggage.

Passengers taking Flight QF400 or above，after going through your immigration procedures，please collect your checked baggage and proceed for inspection by the Australian customs，after this you can proceed to complete the transit procedures.

Please pay attention to the flight information board of the airport to see if there is any change in the Boarding Gate of your next flight. Thank you!

澳大利亚中转提醒

时间：着陆前 25 分钟

女士们、先生们：

乘坐澳洲航空公司 QF399 或 399 以内航班号的旅客，下机后，请按照候机楼内的指示方向，直接办理转机手续，您可以不用提取托运行李。

乘坐 QF400 或 QF400 以上航班号的旅客，办理完入境手续后，请提取所有的托运行李，通过澳大利亚海关的检查，然后办理转机手续。

为确保顺利成行，建议您关注机场实时信息，看您下一段航班的登机口是否有变化。谢谢！

五、补充阅读

Aircraft transfer process（飞机中转转机流程）

Intermediate airport transfer，follow-up flight procedures are the same，need to handle check-in procedures，security check（airport transfer can no longer carry out security check). There are two cases of transit.

The first kind: (1) The flight before and after the flight is the same airline, this situation is more convenient, when handling the first flight, you can request to go through the procedures for the next flight together, the baggage that needs to be checked can also be checked to the end, there is no need to collect the baggage at the intermediate airport, and then check. (2) When you get off the plane at the transit airport, you will be met by the staff of the airline company and arranged to wait at the boarding gate of the subsequent flight. (Big airlines: China Southern, Air China, China Eastern, etc.), and if the previous flight is late, there will be better arrangements. So if possible, should try to choose the same airline flight, make a transfer.

The second kind: If you have a different flight from different airlines, this situation is a little more troublesome. After the arrival of the previous flight, you should go to the transfer counter to go through the formalities for the subsequent flight after you get off the plane normally(small airports generally do not set up the transfer counter, you need to go through the formalities for the subsequent flight after you leave the airport). If you have checked baggage, you need to take it out first and check it again.

在中间机场进行转机，与后续航班的流程是一样的，需要办理值机手续，进行安全检查（机场内中转可以不再进行安全检查）。中转有二种情况。

第一种：

（1）前后航程都是同一个航空公司的航班，这种情况比较方便，在办理第一个航程的时候，就可以要求一并办理下一个航程的手续，需要托运的行李也可以一并托运到底，不需要在中间机场领取行李后，再进行托运。

（2）到达中转机场下机后，会有航空公司的人员接，安排到后续的航班登机口候机。（大型航空公司：南航、国航、东航等），而且如果前面的航班晚点，也会有比较好的安排。所以在可能的情况下，应尽量选择同一个航空公司的航班进行中转。

第二种：

前后航程不是同一个航空公司的航班，这种情况就麻烦一些。前面的航班到达、正常下飞机后，您需要找中转柜台去办理后续航班的手续（小型机场一般不设中转柜台，需要出机场再进行后续航班的手续办理），如果有托运行李，还需要先将行李取出，再进行托运。

项目小结

在飞机着陆阶段，乘务员应对着陆、滑行、下机、转机四个方面进行广播，以此来提醒旅客注意安全，帮助旅客顺利下机和顺利转机。

在客舱广播过程中，可以创造良好的服务氛围，给旅客带来轻松、愉悦、舒适之感，使旅客能够通过客舱广播对空中乘务的工作内容有一个更清晰明确的认识，确保广大旅客能够积极配合空中乘务人员的各项工作。空中乘务人员通过客舱广播，能够有效提升同旅客之间的沟通成果，构建一个良性服务系统，使空中服务协调、统一。

项目训练

1. 在航班出现延误的情况下，提醒旅客做好登机准备，根据这个情境，小组拟写一份广播词并在课上进行播报展示。

项　　目	考核要点	完成情况	评定等级
客舱广播	播报及时		
	播报语气适当		
	广播词格式符合规范		
	广播词表达准确		
	语音音量适中		
	语调生动		
综合评定等级			

2. 小组合作，自设情景（着陆、滑行、下机和转机四个情境）并合理运用客舱广播用语，拍成视频，上传到班级 QQ 群中。

项目六　飞行中特殊情况服务广播

项目目标

○ **知识目标**

　　了解飞行中特殊情况服务广播词的情境和意义；

　　掌握飞行中特殊情况服务广播词的单词和句型；

　　熟练掌握飞行中特殊情况服务广播词和对话等交际用语。

○ **能力目标**

　　通过对飞行中特殊情况服务广播词的理论知识的学习，端正服务态度，培养民航服务意识，做好对客服务的心理准备、思想准备和行为准备。

○ **素质目标**

　　掌握飞行中特殊情况广播词的语言规范要求，提高自身文化修养。

知识框架

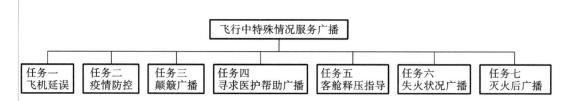

任务一　飞机延误

一、常用词汇和表达

aircraft late arrival　飞机晚点到达

bad/unfavorable weather conditions　恶劣/不利的天气条件

air traffic control　空中交通管制

airport runway congestion　机场跑道拥挤

mechanical problems　机械故障

scheduled　v. 预定的
unfavorable　adj. 不利的
hold-up　举起，抬起
irritating　adj. 令人不快的
alternate　adj. 交替的，轮流的
accommodation　n. 住处，住宿
minor　adj. 较小的
maintenance　n. 维持，维修
staff　n. 职员
diligently　adv. 勤勉地
solve　v. 解决
deicing　n. 除冰
prior to　在……之前
over night　一整夜的
cancel　v. 取消
compensation　n. 赔偿，补偿
specify　v. 细说明，指定，阐述
reimbursement　n. 赔偿；偿付
rerouting　v. 改变线路
well-run　adj. 经营良好的
afford　v. 花费得起；承担得起（后果）
spare　adj. 备用的；多余的；闲置
unforeseen　adj. 无法预料的
technical　adj. 技术的；专业的
operator　n. 操作员
inevitably　adv. 不可避免地
cumulative　adj. 累积的；渐增的；累计的
defect　n. 缺点；缺陷
problematic　adj. 问题的；有疑问的
congest　v. 使充满；使拥挤
off-load　n. 卸货
engross　v. 使全神贯注
withstand　v. 经受住；禁得起
blizzard　n. 暴风雪，大风雪
hurricane　n. 飓风；暴风
tornado　n. 龙卷风；旋风
microburst　n. 微下击暴流
vicinity　n. 邻近，附近；近处
subject to　使服从；受……管制
Federal Aviation Administration(FAA)　美国联邦航空管理局

entitle to　拥有……的权利
stipulated time　约定期限

二、句型练习

We have to wait till the fog lifts.
我们得等到雾散去。
We can't take off because...
我们不能起飞因为……
I'm afraid we have to wait until...
恐怕我们得等到……
We're waiting for the clearance from the air traffic control tower.
我们在等空中交通管制塔的许可。
The ice on the runway has been cleared.
跑道上的冰已被清除。
The aircraft ahead of us to take off.
我们前面要起飞的飞机。
The airport is closed due to poor visibility.
机场因能见度低而关闭。
We'll be leaving as soon as boarding is completed.
我们一登机就走。
Thank you for your patience.
谢谢您的耐心。
Thank you for your understanding and cooperation.
感谢您的理解与合作。

三、对话练习

1

PAX:Excuse me,Miss. Why aren't we leaving yet? It's already past the scheduled departure time.
旅客:不好意思,小姐。为什么我们还不走? 已经过了预定的起飞时间了。
CA:I'm awfully sorry to tell you that our fight has been delayed due to the unfavorable weather conditions.
乘务员:非常抱歉地告诉您,我们的航班因天气状况不佳而延误了。
PAX:You must be kidding. It is sunny outside.
旅客:你一定在开玩笑吧。外面阳光明媚。
CA:Yes Sir. The weather conditions are fine over our airport,but they are unfavorable on flight route. For the sake of safety,we have to wait for the further weather report.

乘务员：是的，先生。机场天气状况良好，但是飞行路线上的天气状况不佳。为了安全起见，我们不得不等待进一步的天气预报。

PAX：How long are we going to wait here?

旅客：我们要在这里等多久？

CA：I'm afraid we have to wait until the weather improves.

乘务员：恐怕我们得等到天气好转。

PAX：That's too bad! I do hope the plane will take off soon.

旅客：那太糟糕了！我真希望飞机能快点起飞。

2

PAX：Miss! Could you come here a second?

旅客：小姐！你能过来一下吗？

CA：What's the matter?

乘务员：怎么了？

PAX：How long has the flight been delayed? When will we be landing on earth?

旅客：航班延误了多长时间？我们什么时候降落？

CA：I'm sorry. We have been delayed for about two and a half hours. We still have another 90 minutes to fly.

乘务员：抱歉。我们延误了大约两个半小时。我们还有90分钟的飞行时间。

PAX：OMG. Could you tell me what the weather will be like when we arrive at the destination?

旅客：天哪。你能告诉我到达的时候天气会是怎样的吗？

CA：According to the present weather report, it is 3 degrees below zero and it's snowing there.

乘务员：根据目前的天气预报，现在是零下3度，那里正在下雪。

PAX：Will the snow let up before our arrival?

旅客：在我们到达之前，雪会减弱吗？

CA：No. The weather forecast says it's going to snow all day.

乘务员：不会。天气预报说要下一整天的雪。

PAX：What a bore!

旅客：真令人厌烦！

CA：Well, perhaps you'll have a white Christmas there.

乘务员：嗯，也许你会在那里过一个白色的圣诞节。

PAX：Yes. That will be terrific.

旅客：是的，那就太棒了！

3

PAX：Miss, I'm sorry to trouble you, but I've got a question.

旅客：小姐，很抱歉打扰你，我有一个问题。

CA：Yes. What can I do for you?

乘务员：我能为您做些什么？

PAX:You see Beijing is my transit airport and I have a connecting flight to Xi'an there. But it seems that our fight could not reach Beijing on time. I will fail to catch my connecting flight. So could you tell me what I can do about my connecting flight?

旅客:北京是我的中转机场,我在那里有一班飞往西安的转机航班,但我们的航班似乎不能按时抵达北京,我将赶不上转机航班。你能告诉我关于转机我能做些什么吗?

CA:I am awfully sorry about the inconvenience caused by the delay. As far as I know,if you miss an onward connecting flight due to our fault,you'll be arranged to take the next available flight to the destination.

乘务员:因延误造成的不便,我深表歉意。据我所知,如果您因为我们的过错而错过了转机航班,我们会安排您乘下一班有空位的航班去目的地。

PAX:Thank you!

旅客:谢谢!

四、广播词

1 Mechanical Problems(机械故障)

ladies and gentlemen,

This is your(chief)purser speaking. The captain has informed us/that our departure will be delayed/due to a minor mechanical problem/with this aircraft. Our maintenance staff is working diligently/to solve this problem. As your safety is our primary concern, please remain in your seat. Further information/will be given/as soon as possible.

Thank you for your understanding and patience.

女士们、先生们:

我是本次航班的(首席)乘务长。机长已通知我们,由于这架飞机的一个小机械故障,我们将推迟起飞。我们的维修人员正在努力解决这个问题。您的安全是我们最关心的问题,请您待在座位上。进一步的信息将尽快提供。

感谢您的理解和耐心。

2 Deicing Delay(除冰延误)

Ladies and gentlemen,

This is your purser speaking. The captain has informed us that this aircraft will need deicing prior to departure. Our ground staff is working diligently on this, please remain in your seat.

Thank you for your understanding!

女士们、先生们:

我是乘务长。机长通知我们,这架飞机起飞前需要除冰。我们的地勤人员正在为此努力工作,请您待在座位上。谢谢您的理解!

3 Waiting For Take-off(等待起飞)

Ladies and gentlemen,

This is your purser speaking. The captain has informed us that due to air traffic control/there are still _____ aircraft currently waiting ahead of us, the departure time will be in approximately 35 minutes. Further information will be given as soon as possible. (We will be serving beverage during this period.)

Thank you for your patience!

女士们、先生们：

我是您的乘务长。机长已通知我们由于空中交通管制/目前有_____飞机在我们前面等候，飞机将在大约35分钟后起飞。后续信息将尽快通知您。（在此期间我们将提供饮料。）

感谢您的耐心！

五、补充阅读

Types of Flight Delay(航班延误的类型)

日前，英国民航局（CAA）根据欧盟委员会关于航班延误或取消的指南，发布了关于航班取消或延误补偿的最新要求，规定任何机械原因导致备降或返航；飞机进行了正常维护，但起飞前发现机械故障；员工罢工（例如空管罢工）等"特殊情况"航空公司不需要对旅客进行补偿。

有部分读者对英国民航局将部分机械原因、员工罢工等列为特殊情况提出了质疑：机械故障不应该属于航空公司原因吗？不应该对旅客进行补偿吗？

关于航班延误的原因，国际上一般将其分为可控原因和不可控原因两种。欧盟指南、英国民航局所指的"特殊情况"，是指航班延误的不可控原因。"特殊情况"表明该情况已经超出了航空公司的控制范畴，欧盟指南规定"特殊情况"需满足三大原则：不可预计、不可避免、外部因素。我国《民法通则》第一百五十三条也有类似规定："不可抗力，是指不能预见、不能避免并不能克服的客观情况。"那么，导致航班延误的天气原因、空中管制原因、机场原因、旅客原因、罢工、航空公司方面的原因等，哪些属于承运人不能预见、不能避免、不能克服的不可抗力、不可控原因呢？

1 Weather(天气原因)

Weather conditions are the objective conditions that the carrier can not foresee, can not avoid and can not overcome.

天气情况是承运人不能预见、不能避免并且不能克服的客观情况。

2 Air Traffic Control(空中管制)

Air traffic control as a force majeure, all flights must comply with the air control, not the carrier can control and change.

空中管制当属于不可抗力，所有航班的飞行都必须遵守空中管制，不是承运人可以控制和改变的。

3 Airport Reason（机场原因）

The carrier and airport signed a service agreement, the aircraft landing site, logistics passenger traffic and other services are provided by the airport. If it is because of the weak airport logistics support led to flight delays, in accordance with the provisions of China's contract law Article 121, a party due to the third party caused by default shall bear the liability for breach of contract to the other party. The disputes between the second party and the third party, in accordance with the provisions of law or in accordance with the agreed solution, the carrier shall undertake the responsibility of breach of flight delays to the passenger, and can not claim force majeure, exclude airport outside the party in violation of the service agreement, the carrier can not see, unavoidable and insurmountable such as the closure of the airport, security problems belong to force majeure category.

承运人与机场签订了服务协议，由机场提供飞机起落场地、后勤保障、旅客通行等服务，如果是因为机场后勤保障不力导致航班延误的，依照我国《合同法》第一百二十一条的规定，即"当事人一方因第三方的原因造成违约的，应当向对方承担违约责任。当事人一方和第三方之间的纠纷，依照法律规定或者按照约定解决"，承运人应向旅客承担航班延误的违约责任，而不能主张不可抗力；除机场一方违反服务约定的情况外，承运人不能预见、不能避免并不能克服的诸如机场关闭、安检问题等则属于不可抗力范畴。

4 Passenger Reason（旅客原因）

Due to the flight delays caused by passengers themselves, not only can not be held responsible for liability for breach of contract, but may be due to their own reasons and should make compensation to other passengers.

因旅客自身原因而导致的航班延误，不但不能追究承运人的违约责任，反而有可能因旅客自身原因而向其他旅客作出赔偿。

5 Strike（罢工）

Strikes are objective phenomenon can not be accurately predicted. Although carrier can foresee to a certain extent, but can not accurately and promptly foresee the time, place, the continuation of the time and range of objective phenomenon. Therefore, it still belongs to the category of unforeseen, belongs to the force majeure.

罢工属于不能准确预见的客观现象。对于罢工，承运人虽有一定程度的预见，但并不能准确、及时地预见发生的时间、地点、延续时间、影响范围等，因此仍属于不能预见的范畴，属于不可抗力。

6 Airlines Reasons（航空公司原因）

The main reasons for the airlines are：

(1) flight schedule is too full(including the sale), the lack of capacity backup.

(2) flight schedule is not reasonable.

(3) the allocation of the unit is not timely.

(4) mechanical failure, etc.

航空公司方面的原因主要有：

(1) 航班安排过满（包括超售），运力备份不足。

(2) 航班计划安排不合理。

(3) 机组调配不及时。

(4) 机械故障等。

Exercise（练习）

1. Please fill in the blanks with the appropriate words.

(1) I'm sorry, but something has gone wrong with the plane. The flight will have to be _____.

(2) We regret to announce that your arrival time will be _____ to 9 p.m..

(3) We plan to go to picnic today, but it's raining, How _____.

(4) There are many reasons for _____ for example, bad weather conditions.

2. Please fill in the blanks with the exact words or phrases according to the first letter.

Flight delays are p _____ of air travel because aircraft operate in f _____ exposure to the weather, especially in the weather-related winter. In a _____, although the aircraft is reliable, the parts may wear out, and w _____ they wear out, the delay may be extended to a few days. The question is n _____ that there are, but more is "how do airlines deal with passengers in the f _____ of flight delays?" Regardless of the e _____ of flight delays, airlines have the right to let p _____ know what a delay is and when it is likely to be delayed, no matter how many hours or minutes it is.

任务二　疫情防控

一、常用词汇和表达

Novel Coronavirus　新型冠状病毒

pneumonia　n. 肺炎

route of transmission　传播途径

close contact　密切接触者

epidemic　n. 流行病

outbreak　v. 爆发

contagion　n. 接触传染

fever, cough and difficulty in breathing　发热、咳嗽、呼吸困难

medical supplies　医疗物资
quarantine　n./v.隔离,检疫
mask　n.口罩
surgical mask　医用外科口罩
protective clothing　防护服
eye shields,goggles　护目镜
shoe covers　鞋套
gloves　手套
disposable　adj.一次性
to wear　穿戴
to remove　祛除
disinfection　n.消毒
disinfectant　n.消毒剂
chlorinated disinfectant　含氯消毒液
alcohol　n.酒精
to spray　喷洒
hand sanitizer,liquid soap　洗手液
disposable gloves　一次性手套

二、句型练习

1. During the epidemic, please wear a mask and pay attention to personal protection.
疫情期间请戴好口罩,注意个人防护。
2. For everyone's safety, please do not take off the mask in the cabin.
为了大家的安全,请不要在客舱内摘下口罩。
3. Please cooperate with the staff to take the temperature and spray alcohol for disinfection.
请配合工作人员测量体温,喷洒酒精进行消毒。
4. Please cooperate with the epidemic prevention work to fill in the health declaration form.
请配合疫情防护工作,填写健康申报表。
5. Please pay attention to personal protection.
请注意个人防护。

三、对话练习

CA:Excuse me, sir. Please don't take off your mask in the cabin.
乘务员:不好意思,先生。请不要在客舱内摘下口罩。
PAX:Oh. But I've been wearing a mask for too long and I don't feel very well.

旅客:哦。但是我戴口罩太久了,感觉不太舒服。

CA:I'm sorry, during the epidemic, please cooperate with our work and do personal protection.

乘务员:很抱歉,在疫情期间,请配合我们的工作,做好个人防护。

PAX:Okay, I'll put on my mask right away.

旅客:好的,我马上戴上口罩。

CA:Thank you for your understanding and cooperation.

乘务员:感谢您的理解和配合。

四、广播词

Ladies and gentlemen,

The cabin crew will distribute the health declaration forms and entry card right now. Please fill in the related forms and submit them to customs officials. You will be not allowed to enter Myanmar if you have not filled in these forms. All passengers should have home quarantine for 2 weeks after arrival. Thank you for your cooperation.

女士们、先生们:

现在乘务员将为您发放健康申报表及入境卡,请您在飞机上完成填写,并在落地后交给海关检疫官员。未申报者将被拒绝进入缅甸。在您入境后,还需配合当地检疫要求,居家隔离 14 天。感谢您的配合。

Ladies and gentlemen,

Good morning! Welcome aboard CA889. It is our pleasure to greet you again. All the crew members express our sincere greetings to you.

During the epidemic, please wear a mask, do personal protection, and follow the instructions and arrangements of the flight attendants. The cabin service standards are adjusted, while our passion and care will never change. We thank you for your understanding and cooperation.

女士们、先生们:

早上好!欢迎乘坐 CA889 航班。很高兴与您再次见面,我们全体机组人员向您致以诚挚的问候。

疫情期间,请戴好口罩,做好个人防护,听从乘务员的指挥和安排。客舱服务标准会有所改调整,但我们的热情和关怀是不会改变的,感谢您的理解和配合。

五、补充阅读

According to the notice of the municipal epidemic prevention and control headquarters, from now on, all passengers arriving at Zhuhai Airport are required to carry out landing nucleic acid testing. The specific measures are as follows:

1. All arriving passengers must wear masks correctly, cooperate with the inspection of Yuekang green code and nearly 14-day itinerary, cooperate with the on-site staff to measure the temperature, and carry out landing nucleic acid testing before they can leave.

2. Passengers with red and yellow codes, passengers with abnormal body temperature, and passengers arriving in cities with medium and high risk areas in the past 14 days must be handed over to the jurisdiction for disposal.

3. The regional epidemic risk level is adjusted dynamically. Passengers can scan the code and enter the Mini Program of the State Council client to inquire about the regional epidemic risk level.

根据市疫情防控指挥部通知,即日起,所有到达珠海机场的旅客均须进行落地核酸检测。具体措施如下:

1. 所有到达旅客须正确佩戴口罩,配合查验粤康码绿码和近14日行程轨迹,配合现场工作人员测温,进行落地核酸检测后方可离开。

2. 持红黄码旅客、体温异常旅客、近14日有中高风险地区所在地市行程轨迹的到达旅客,均须移交辖区处置。

3. 地区疫情风险等级动态调整,各位旅客可扫码进入国务院客户端小程序查询地区疫情风险等级。

Exercise(练习)

Please fill in the blanks with the appropriate words.

1. Please wear a _____ during the epidemic.
2. Please cooperate with the measurement of body _____.
3. Please pay attention to personal safety _____.

任务三　颠簸广播

一、常用词汇和表达

turbulence　n.湍流
moderate turbulence　中等湍流
severe turbulence　严重湍流
sudden turbulence　突然的湍流
airsick　adj.晕机的
airsickness bag　晕机袋
waste bag　垃圾袋
seat pocket　座椅口袋

vomit   v. 呕吐
fasten the seat belt   系好安全带
keep seat belt fastened   系好安全带
seat belt sign   安全带指示灯
return to your seat   回到您的座位上
remain in your seat   待在您的座位上

二、句型练习

If you feel airsick, please use the airsickness bag.
如果您感到晕机,请使用晕机袋。
Refrain from using the lavatories until the seat belt sign goes off.
在安全带指示灯熄灭前不要使用洗手间。
Lavatories may not be used at this time.
此时不得使用洗手间。
When you are using the lavatory, please hold the handle tightly.
使用洗手间时,请您握紧把手。
Our aircraft is experiencing some moderate rough air and it is expected to last for some time.
我们的飞机遇到了一些中等强度的气流,预计会持续一段时间。
We advise you to keep your seat belt fastened as a precaution against sudden turbulence.
我们建议您系好安全带,以防突然的湍流。
Our plane is very bumpy at the present. Please keep your seat belt fastened/Please be seated and fasten your seat belt.
我们的飞机目前很颠簸。请系好安全带/请坐下并系好安全带。
Please take extra care if you are having meals.
吃饭时请格外小心。
For the time being, cabin service will be suspended.
暂时停止客舱服务。
We apologize for the inconvenience caused.
给您带来的不便,我们深表歉意。
If you have any concerns, please contact our flight attendants.
如果您有任何问题,请联系我们的乘务员。
Thank you for your understanding.
谢谢您的理解。
Thank you for your cooperation.
谢谢您的合作。

三、对话练习

1

CA：Excuse me, sir, the seat belt sign is still on. Please keep the seat belt fastened.

乘务员：不好意思,先生,安全带指示灯还亮着,请系好安全带。

PAX：Yes, I know. I'm strapped in.

旅客：是的,我知道,我正在系。

CA：Your son must be strapped in, too.

乘务员：您的儿子也要系上安全带。

PAX：I can hold him on my lap.

旅客：我可以把他抱在我的腿上。

CA：I'm sorry, sir. It's not secure for him. You have to use the extension belt. Let me help you.

乘务员：对不起,先生。这对他来说不太安全。您必须使用延长带。让我来帮您。

PAX：Oh, for God's sake! He'll scream the place down.

旅客：哦,看在上帝的分上!他会尖叫着把这个地方夷为平地。

CA：Sir, we will experience some turbulence very soon. Strap him in now. It's for his safety.

乘务员：先生,我们预计很快会遇到湍流。现在给他系上安全带,是为了他的安全。

PAX：All right. I will do it.

旅客：好的,我会做的。

2

CA：Yes, Madam. Is there anything I can do for you?

乘务员：是的,女士。有什么我能为您效劳的吗?

PAX：When will you provide meal service?

旅客：你们什么时候提供餐饮服务?

CA：We've been informed by our captain just now, we'll meet some strong headwinds, so there will be moderate to severe turbulence. If that happens, the meal service will be delayed. I suggest you to fasten your seat belt for any unforeseen turbulence. After that, we'll start meal service.

乘务员：我们的机长刚刚通知我们,我们将遇到一些强烈的逆风,因此将会产生中度到严重的湍流。如果发生这种情况,餐饮服务将被推迟。我建议您系好安全带,以防意外湍流。之后,我们将开始提供餐饮服务。

PAX：I see.

旅客：我明白了。

CA：Ladies and gentlemen, we are entering an area of turbulence. So please fasten your seat belts, use of the lavatories has been suspended. (To a passenger standing in the aisle) Sir, please return to your seat.

乘务员：女士们、先生们，我们正在进入一个湍流区域。请系好安全带，厕所已暂停使用。（对站在过道上的旅客说）先生，请回到您的座位上。

四、广播词

Turbulence 1（湍流 1）

Ladies and gentlemen,

We are encountering turbulence. For your safety and comfort, please remain seated and fasten your seat belt. Toilets are not in use. If you feel airsick, please use the airsickness bag located in the seat pocket in front of you.

Cabin service will be suspended during this period.

Thank you.

女士们、先生们：

我们遇到了湍流。为了您的安全和舒适，请您坐好，系好安全带。厕所不能使用。如果您感到晕机，请使用您前面袋子里的晕机包。

在此期间，客舱服务将暂停。

谢谢。

Turbulence 2（湍流 2）

Ladies and gentlemen,

We are experiencing some turbulence. For your safety, please return to your seat and fasten your seat belt. Please avoid using the toilets at this time. Cabin service will be suspended during this period.

Thank you.

女士们、先生们：

我们遇到了一些湍流。为了您的安全，请回到您的座位上并系好安全带。请不要在这个时候使用厕所。

在此期间，客舱服务将暂停。

谢谢。

Turbulence 3（湍流 3）

Ladies and gentlemen,

Our aircraft is experiencing some turbulence. Please be seated as soon as possible and fasten your seat belt. Do not use the lavatories. And we regret that we are unable to serve you at this time. Please take extra care while taking your meals.

Thank you.

女士们、先生们：

我们的飞机遇到了一些湍流。请您尽快就座并系好安全带。不要使用厕所。很抱歉，我们现在不能为您服务。用餐时请格外小心。

谢谢。

Turbulence 4(Suspension of cabin service)湍流 4(客舱服务暂停)

Ladies and gentlemen,

We are currently experiencing some turbulence. For your safety, please return to your seat and fasten your seat belt. Refrain from using the lavatories until the seat belt sign goes off. Cabin service will be suspended during this time.

Thank you for your understanding.

女士们、先生们：

我们现在遇到了一些湍流。为了您的安全，请回到您的座位上并系好安全带。在安全带指示灯熄灭之前，不要使用厕所。客舱服务将在此期间暂停。

谢谢您的理解。

Moderate Turbulence(中度湍流)

Ladies and gentlemen,

Our aircraft is experiencing some moderate turbulence and it is expected to last for some time. The captain has informed us that we will pass through an area of rough air in _____ minutes, and the moderate turbulence will last for _____ minutes.

Please be seated and fasten your seat belt. Do not use the lavatories. Please take extra care if you are having meals. For the time being, cabin service will be suspended.

Thank you.

女士们、先生们：

我们的飞机遇到了中度湍流，预计还会持续一段时间。机长通知我们，我们将在_____分钟后穿过一片扰动气流，中度湍流将持续_____分钟。

请您坐好并系好安全带。不要使用厕所。如果您正在用餐，请格外小心。客舱服务将暂停。

谢谢。

Severe Turbulence(严重湍流)

Ladies and gentlemen,

We have encountered some strong turbulence. Please take your seat and fasten your seat belt. Do not use the lavatories.

Cabin service will be suspended during this period.

女士们、先生们：

我们遇到了一些强烈的湍流。请您坐好并系好安全带。不要使用厕所。客舱服务将在此期间暂停。

After Severe Turbulence(在严重湍流之后)

Ladies and gentlemen,

The aircraft has experienced some severe turbulence. We apologize for the inconvenience caused. If you have any problems, please contact us.

Thank you for your understanding and cooperation.

女士们、先生们：

飞机经历了严重湍流。给您带来的不便，我们深表歉意。如果您有任何问题，请与我们联系。

感谢您的理解和合作。

五、补充阅读

（一）Public Address System（公共广播系统）

In an airplane, there is a public address system. This system has a microphone and a loudspeaker which makes it possible to speak to many people at the same time. It is part of the plane's intercom system. There are intercom stations in the passenger cabin as well as in the cockpit, or the pilot's cabin. This allows the pilots of the airline to speak privately to any of the flight attendants. The crew can communicate with the cockpit over the intercom. Passengers or anyone else who is not listening over the headphone of the intercom cannot hear what is being said.

飞机上有一个公共广播系统。这个系统有一个麦克风和一个扩音器，可以同时对许多人讲话。它是飞机内部通信系统的一部分。客舱和驾驶舱或飞行员舱都有对讲机，这使得该航空公司的飞行员可以私下与任何空乘人员交谈。机组人员可以通过对讲机与驾驶舱通信，旅客或其他没有通过对讲机耳机收听的人无法听到广播内容。

（二）Turbulence（湍流）

Turbulence may make people feel uncomfortable, but it is normal. People often misunderstand turbulence. When encountering turbulence, nervous passengers feel the plane is "falling" out of the sky. It is natural for them to only feel the "down" bumps. But for every "down" there bumpy road, imagine you are a passenger on a plane and how you would consider it to be "bad" turbulence. Now take a look at the road. How big are the bumps on the roadway to create the rough ride? The air is usually very smooth. But sometimes some small ripples can make it feel like "bad" turbulence! Wind flowing over obstacles such as mountains can cause turbulence. It is kind of like water flowing in a river with small eddies. A common winter time turbulence occurrence is called "mountain waves". This is produced downwind from a mountain range when the winter jet stream is at a lower altitude. The air mass in the mountain wave will flow up and down a little bit like sea swells. This can cause turbulence and is typical east of the Rocky Mountains. Weather forecasters are very good at predicting this type of turbulence because it is easy to track the location of the jet stream. Airlines may change the cruising altitude to minimize its annoying effects.

Turbulence can also be caused by shifting wind currents in the sky. When you transit from one wind current to another, such as crossing a warm or cold front, the air can get stirred up. Planes flying through these transition areas will normally experience some turbulence.

One of the more common types of turbulence is caused by "convective" heating. As mute the sun warms the ground, the hot air rises and makes the air have a "bumpy" feeling. You may see evidence of this by small puffy shaped clouds. This type of turbulence is normally limited to the lower altitudes.

There are many sources of information about turbulence available to pilots. They get information from the national weather service, company dispatchers and from their own observations of sky and cloud formations.

You might feel "convective" turbulence for a short while after take-off or before landing on hot sunny afternoons. It poses no danger and is rarely classified as anything but light or mild turbulence. Birds such as hawks and eagles use this rising energy of hot air to soar above fields. This way, they avoid having to flap their wings while searching for prey.

湍流可能会让人感到不舒服，但这是正常的。人们经常误解湍流。当遇到气流时，紧张的旅客会觉得飞机正在从空中"坠落"。对他们来说，只感到"向下"的颠簸是很自然的。但是对于每一条崎岖的道路，想象一下你是飞机上的一名旅客，你会如何看待这些"糟糕的"乱流。现在看一看路，道路上的湍流有多大才会造成颠簸？空气通常很平稳，但有时一些小涟漪会让你感觉像是"糟糕的"湍流！风经过山脉之类的障碍物会引起湍流，它有点像水流在河里产生的小漩涡。一种常见的冬季湍流现象被称为"山脉波动"。这是冬季急流在较低的高度时从山脉的顺风处产生的。山脉波动中的气团会像海浪一样上下波动。这可能会引起湍流，这是落基山脉东部的典型现象。天气预报员非常擅长预测这种类型的湍流，因为很容易跟踪急流的位置。航空公司可能会改变巡航高度，以减少其恼人的影响。

气流的变化也会引起湍流。当你从一股气流转移到另一股气流时，比如穿过暖锋或冷锋时，空气就会被搅动起来。在这些过渡区域飞行的飞机通常会遇到一些湍流。

其中一种更常见的湍流是由"对流"加热引起的。当太阳使地面变暖时，热空气上升，使空气有一种"颠簸"的感觉。你可以从蓬松的小云层中看出来。这种类型的湍流通常只出现在较低的高度。

对飞行员来说，有很多关于湍流的信息来源。他们从国家气象局、公司调度员以及他们自己对天空和云层形成的观察中获取信息。

在炎热晴朗的下午，你可能会在起飞后或着陆前的短时间内感到"对流"湍流。它不构成危险，只是被归类为轻微的湍流。鹰等鸟类利用热空气上升的能量在田野上空翱翔，这样就可以避免在寻找猎物时拍打翅膀。

（三）Reasons for the turbulence（湍流的原因）

The plane is bumping because there is turbulence in the atmosphere. These unstable airflows vary in range, direction, and velocity. When an aircraft enters a turbulence vortex similar to the size of the body, each part of the aircraft will be affected by airflow in different directions and speeds, and the original balance of aerodynamic force and torque will be destroyed, thus producing irregular movement. When an airplane moves from one vortex to another, it vibrates. When the aircraft's natural vibration period is comparable to the turbulence pulsation period, the turbulence becomes very intense.

According to the intensity of turbulence, it can be classified as light, moderate and heavy turbulence. Light turbulence means that the person in the seat may feel a slight stress on the seat belt or shoulder straps, and unsecured objects may be slightly moved, with little difficulty in walking and without affecting cabin service. Moderate turbulence occurs when the seat belt or shoulder straps are felt by the person in the seat, 80% of the drink is spilling from the glass, cabin service is affected, mobility in the cabin is difficult, and unsecured objects are moved. Heavy turbulence means that the person in the seat feels the heavy force on the seat belt or shoulder straps, and the object swings back and forth from side to side and is thrown up. Cabin service is not available.

In the event of turbulence, the flight crew and the cabin crew have their own contingency plans and operating procedures. The crew will adjust the appropriate travel speed to avoid the aircraft to bear a large load, in accordance with the program to complete the specified action. At the same time, the seat belt signal light will be switched on to remind passengers to fasten their seat belts. The flight attendant will broadcast in time to remind the passengers standing in the cabin to return to their seats and fasten their seat belts. The use of the restroom will be suspended. In case of slight turbulence, service will continue, but no hot drinks will be provided to avoid scalding passengers. In case of moderate turbulence, the cabin crew will immediately terminate the service and push the dining car and beverage car back to the kitchen. In case of severe turbulence, the flight attendant should immediately put the brake on the spot, put the hot drink pot in the drink car, and sit nearby and fasten the seat belt.

飞机产生颠簸,是由于大气中存在湍流。这些不稳定气流的范围、方向和速度各不相同。当飞机进入与机体尺寸相近的湍流涡旋时,飞机的各部位就会受到不同方向和速度的气流影响,原有的空气动力和力矩的平衡被破坏,从而产生不规则的运动。飞机由一个涡旋进入另一个涡旋,就会引起振动。当飞机的自然振动周期与湍流脉动周期相当时,飞机颠簸就会变得十分强烈。

以湍流的强度分类,可分为轻度湍流、中度湍流和重度湍流。轻度湍流是指在座位上的人员可能感觉到安全带或者肩带轻微受力,未固定的物体可能有轻微移动,行走几乎没有困难,不影响客舱服务。中度湍流是指在座位上的人员能感到安全带或肩带的受力,八成满的饮料会从杯中溅出来,客舱服务会受到影响,客舱内走动困难,未固定的物体会移动。重度湍流是指在座位上的人员感到安全带或肩带猛烈受力,未固定的物体前后左右摆动、抛起。无法进行客舱服务。

发生湍流时,飞行机组和乘务组都有相应的预案和操作程序。机组会调整合适的飞行速度,避免飞机承受较大载荷,按照程序完成规定的动作。同时还会打开安全带信号灯,提醒旅客系好安全带。乘务员会及时广播,提醒在客舱中站着的旅客回到座位坐好,系好安全带,洗手间将暂停使用。轻微湍流时,乘务员会继续服务,但不提供热饮,避免烫伤旅客。

中度湍流时,乘务组会立即终止服务,将餐车、饮料车推回厨房。重度湍流时,乘务员应立即原地踩刹车,将热饮壶放置在饮料车内,并就近坐好,系好安全带。

任务四　寻求医护帮助广播

一、常用词汇和表达

fever　n. 发烧
headache　n. 头痛
stomachache　n. 胃痛
toothache　n. 牙疼
nose bleed　鼻出血
running nose　流鼻涕
painkiller　n. 止疼药
bandage　n. 绷带
gauze　n. 纱布
pressure　n. 压力
unfasten　v. 解开
jolt　n. 颠簸,摇晃
bump　n. 肿块,隆起物
forehead　n. 前额
wrap　v. 包扎
ankle　n. 脚踝
sprain　v. 扭伤
ear ringing　耳鸣
swallow　v. 吞咽
sore　adj. 疼痛的
stuff　vt. 堵塞
aspirin　n. 阿司匹林
nap　n. 打盹儿

二、句型练习

Do you feel dizzy?
您觉得头晕吗?
Are you feeling better?
您感觉好些了吗?

Are you allergic to any medicine?

您对什么药过敏吗?

Do you suffer from high blood pressure?

您有高血压吗?

Have you brought any medicine yourself?

您自己带药了吗?

Do you have a stomachache/headache/toothache?

您胃痛/头痛/牙痛吗?

I'll bring you a cup of warm water immediately.

我马上给您拿杯温水来。

Have you ever suffered from airsickness before?

您以前晕机过吗?

Please tell us if you need any assistance.

如果您需要帮助,请告诉我们。

If you still don't feel well, please don't hesitate to let us know.

如果您还是不舒服,请尽管告诉我们。

Because of a change in air pressure, you are suffering from an earache.

由于气压的变化,您会耳痛。

You may take a nap after taking the medicine, I'll bring you a blanket.

您吃药后可以小睡一会儿,我给您拿条毯子。

三、对话练习

1

PAX: Miss, the plane is bumping badly. I'm very sick and dizzy and I feel like vomiting.

旅客:小姐,飞机颠簸得很厉害。我很难受,头晕目眩,想吐。

CA: Have you ever suffered from airsickness before? You're probably airsick.

乘务员:您以前晕机过吗?您可能是晕机了。

PAX: Airsickness? It's my first time to take a plane. What shall I do now?

旅客:晕机?这是我第一次坐飞机。我现在该怎么办呢?

CA: You may need some airsickness tablets. I'll get you the tablets at once. May I assist you in reclining your seat back so you can have a rest? If you want to vomit, please use the airsickness bag in the seat pocket in front of you. I will attend to it.

乘务员:您可能需要一些晕机药片。我马上给您拿药片来。我可以帮您把座椅靠背向后倾,让您休息一下吗?如果您想呕吐,请使用前面座位口袋里的晕机袋。我会处理这件事的。

PAX: That's very kind of you.

旅客:你真是太好了!

2

PAX:Help!

旅客:救命!

CA:What's the matter with you,sir?

乘务员:先生,您怎么了?

PAX:I was going to the lavatory. There was a sudden jolt and I fell down and hurt myself.

旅客:我正要去洗手间。突然一阵颠簸,我摔倒了,伤到了自己。

CA:You've got a bump on your forehead,and some cuts here.

乘务员:您额头上有个肿块,这里有几处伤口。

PAX:Really? Am I bleeding?

旅客:真的吗? 我在流血吗?

CA:Don't worry. The bleeding is controlled. Let's wash the cuts. I'll wrap it up with gauze. Would you please sit down and have a rest?

乘务员:别担心。血已经止住了。我们把伤口清洗一下吧。我会用纱布包起来的。请您坐下来休息一下好吗?

PAX:Ouch! My right ankle is hurting! It must be sprained top!

旅客:哎呀! 我的右脚踝疼! 一定是扭伤了!

CA:If your right ankle is sprained,we will try to contact a doctor among our passengers. However,if that happens to be no doctor on board,we'll assist you to move to the rear cabin. There are some vacant seats there. I'll lift up the armrests so that you can sit down.

乘务员:如果您的右脚踝扭伤了,我们会试着去旅客中找医生。但是,如果飞机上没有医生,我们会帮您移到后舱,那里有一些空位。我会把扶手抬起来,这样您就可以坐了。

PAX:That will be great.

旅客:那就太好了。

3

PAX:Miss,my ears are ringing after take-off. It really hurts. What's wrong with me?

旅客:小姐,起飞后我的耳朵都响了,真的很疼。我哪儿出问题了?

CA:Don't worry. Because of a change in air pressure,you are suffering from an earache. You can relieve your earache by swallowing and by eating sweets. And you'll feel better when the plane stops climbing.

乘务员:别担心。因为气压的变化,您现在耳朵疼。您可以通过吞咽和吃甜食来缓解您的耳朵痛。当飞机停止爬升时,您会感觉好些。

PAX:OK,I will have a try.

旅客:好的,我试一试。

四、广播词

Ladies and gentlemen,

May I have your attention,please?

One of our passengers on board needs immediate medical attention. If you are medical certified professional, please identify yourself to a member of our flight crew. Your assistance will be greatly appreciated.

Thank you.

女士们、先生们：

请注意！

机上一名旅客需要立即就医，如果您是专业医护人员，请向我们的机组人员表明您的身份。非常感谢您的帮助。

谢谢！

Ladies and gentlemen,

Your attention please. We urgently need the assistance of a doctor or nurse. If there are any medical professionals on board, please approach one of the flight attendants as soon as possible.

Thank you for your help!

女士们、先生们：

请注意！我们急需医生或护士的帮助，如果飞机上有哪位旅客是医护人士，请您尽快与乘务员联系。

非常感谢您的帮助！

五、补充阅读

First Aid(急救)

First aid is an assistance given to an injured or sick person in need of urgent medical assistance. First aid consists of not only specific knowledge and skills, but also the abilities to assess a situation and make appropriate decisions. Medical incidents include a broad range of medical situations, from someone feeling queasy to a full-blown heart attack at 37 000 feet. More common situations include passengers vomiting, fainting from lack of oxygen, or needing a bandage or a small cut, to more serious conditions like administering to diabetic shock and epileptic seizure. Most cabin attendants receive training for all of these situations. Sometimes doctors who fly as passengers are liable to be called upon to render first aid in the air. The principle of first aid is immediate action but it is essential that quick action should not cause panic. Any action needs to be careful and deliberate and the first-aid personnel must remain calm at all times.

Two of the most difficult emergencies to encounter in-flight are heart attacks and premature births. Expectant mothers are not supposed to fly close to their due date, but babies are still born on board. On domestic flights, the pilots can usually land before birth, but on transoceanic flights, this is not often an option. All that most cabin attendants in this situation can do is to get hot water and blankets to prevent infection, call for a doctor, and help the passenger push her way to motherhood. Heart attacks are much more common than in-flight childbirth.

Perhaps the most common of all medical assistance is calming the fearful flyer. Usually, nervous flyer feel horribly out of control and don't understand the mechanics of flight. In this case, personal attention, a soothing voice and a compassionate heart help most of the time.

急救是对需要紧急医疗救助的受伤或生病的人的援助。急救不仅包括特定的知识和技能，还包括评估情况和做出适当决定的能力。医疗事故包括一系列医疗情况，从某人感到恶心到在37 000英尺的高空心脏病发作。更常见的情况包括旅客呕吐、缺氧晕倒、需要绷带或出现小伤口，更严重的情况是处理糖尿病休克和癫痫发作。大多数空乘人员都接受过这些情况的培训。有时，作为旅客的医生可能会被要求在空中进行急救。急救的原则是立即行动，但最重要的是迅速行动不能引起恐慌。任何行动都需要小心谨慎，急救人员必须始终保持冷静。

在飞机上遇到的两种最困难的紧急情况是心脏病发作和早产。准妈妈们不应该在预产期前乘飞机，但婴儿还是会在飞机上出生。在国内航班上，飞行员通常可以在孩子出生前将飞机着陆，但在跨洋航班上，这通常不是一个好的选择。在这种情况下，大多数空乘人员能做的就是拿热水和毯子来防止感染，打电话叫医生，帮助旅客成为母亲。而心脏病发作比在飞机上分娩更常见。

也许最常见的医疗援助是安抚情绪受到影响的飞行员。通常，情绪过于紧张的飞行员会感到可怕的失控。在这种情况下，个人关注、舒缓的声音、一颗富有同情心的心大多数时候都能帮助到飞行员。

任务五　客舱释压指导

一、常用词汇和表达

depressurize　vt. 使减压，使降压
loose　adj. 松的，未固定的，零散的
pressure　n. 压力

二、句型练习

1. Please give me your full attention!
请大家注意!
2. The aircraft is now descending due to pressure relief.

由于释压原因，飞机现在正在下降。

3．Please fasten your seat belts and remain calm.

请系好您的安全带，保持冷静。

4．May l have your attention please?

请大家注意了！

5．Thank your for your attention.

谢谢您的收听。

6．We expect to arrive in an hour.

我们预计在1小时后到达。

7．We apologize for any inconvenience.

对此引起的不便，我们表示歉意。

三、对话练习

(To passengers in the cabin)

(致机舱内旅客)

CA：Ladies and gentlemen, due to a mechanical fault, the cabin pressure has reduced. Please pull the oxygen mask over your nose and mouth.

乘务员：女士们、先生们，由于机械故障，机舱压力下降。请将氧气面罩拉到口鼻处。

(To the lady in the cabin who has not put her mask on)

(致机舱内未戴面罩的女士)

CA：Madam, please put your oxygen mask on as quickly as possible.

旅客：女士，请尽快戴上氧气面罩。

PAX：I have to help my son first. He is too young to put it on by himself.

旅客：我得先帮我儿子，他太小了，不能自己戴。

CA：Put your own mask first, please!

乘务员：请先戴上您自己的面罩。

PAX：Thank you for reminding me.

旅客：谢谢你提醒我。

四、广播词

1

Ladies and gentlemen,

Attention! Please sit down immediately. Pull an oxygen mask firmly toward yourself. Place the mask over your nose and mouth and breathe normally.

Put on your own mask first before assisting others.

Please remain seated with your seat belt fastened until further instruction.

女士们、先生们：

请注意！请您立即就座。请用力拉下面罩,罩在口鼻处正常呼吸。

戴好自己的氧气面罩后再去帮助别人。

请大家在下一个指令发出前系好安全带,在自己的座位上坐好。

2
(Informing passengers of cabin depressurization)

Ladies and gentlemen,

Attention, please!

Our aircraft is loosing pressure and is now depressurizing. We will descend due to the loss of pressure. Please follow the instructions of the flight attendants and remain calm.

Thank you.

通知旅客客舱减压

女士们、先生们：

请注意！我们的飞机正在失去压力,现在正在减压。由于紧急失压,我们将下降。请您听从乘务员的指示,保持冷静。

谢谢！

任务六　失火状况广播

一、常用词汇和表达

fire　　n. 火灾,火

contain　　vt. 包含,容纳,克制,遏制,包括

relocate　　vt. & vi. 迁移,重新安置

smoky　　adj. 冒烟的,多烟的,有烟熏味的,烟状的

bend　　vt. (使)弯曲,屈身,拉弯

cover　　v. 遮盖,掩蔽,涉及

handkerchief　　n. 手帕

二、句型练习

1. A minor fire has broken out in the lavatory in the front/center/rear section of the cabin and we are quickly containing the situation.

机舱前部/中部/后部的洗手间发生了小火灾,我们正在迅速控制火势。

2. Pull the oxygen mask firmly toward yourself, place it over your nose and mouth and breathe normally.

用力将氧气面罩拉向自己,放在口鼻处正常呼吸。

三、对话练习

PAX:Hello, what happened?

旅客:你好,发生什么事了?

CA:There is a small fire in the cabin. Please don't panic. We are dealing with it.

乘务员:客舱发生了一场小火灾。请不要惊慌。我们正在处理这件事。

PAX:I'm a little scared. What do we need to do?

旅客:我有点害怕。我们需要做些什么?

CA:Don't worry, we'll take care of it. Please bend down, cover your mouth and nose with your clothes and follow the conductor's instructions.

乘务员:别担心,我们会处理好的。请弯下腰,用衣服遮住口鼻,听从乘务员的指挥。

PAX:OK, I'll do what you say.

旅客:好的,我会按你说的去做。

CA:Now the fire in the cabin has been controlled and the aircraft is in good condition. Thank you for your cooperation.

乘务员:现在机舱内的火势已经得到了控制,飞机状态良好。感谢您的配合。

四、广播词

Ladies and gentlemen,

We are putting out a minor fire that has broken out in the lavatory in the front/center/rear section of the cabin. Passengers sitting in the front/center/rear section, please follow the cabin attendants' directions. All other passengers please do not leave your seats.

女士们、先生们:

现在客舱前部/中部/后部的洗手间失火,我们正在组织灭火,坐在火源附近的旅客,请听从乘务员指挥。其他旅客请坐好,不要离开座位。

Ladies and gentlemen,

Attention, please!

A minor fire has broken out in the lavatory in the front/center/rear section of the cabin and we are containing the situation.

Please keep calm and follow the instructions of flight attendants. We will relocate the passengers sitting near the area of the fire. All other passengers please remain in your seats with your seat belts securely fastened.

Thank you for your cooperation.

女士们、先生们:

请注意!

客舱前/中/后部的洗手间发生了一场小火灾,我们正在控制火势。

请保持冷静,听从乘务员的指挥。我们将重新安排坐在火灾区域附近的旅客。其他旅客请务必留在座位上,系好安全带。

谢谢您的合作。

五、补充阅读

客舱火灾的类型

在客舱内发生的火灾大致分为四类:A 类——纸、布、木类引起的火灾;B 类——油类引起的火灾;C 类——电器引起的火灾;D 类——可燃性固定物质引起的火灾。

(1)纸、木、布引起的一般类型的火灾。这类火灾通常发生在客舱的座椅、衣帽间、行李架,尤其是在冬天,人们所穿戴的尼龙衣物在高空静电、压力等多种环境下会产生火花,从而致燃。预防措施:乘务员应加强理论知识的学习,强化安全意识。乘务员要加大对易燃空间的检查力度,提早发现火灾。处置措施:当这类火灾发生时,乘务员必须迅速取出相应的灭火瓶进行灭火,口头告知就近的乘务员失火的信息,根据处置预案分工合作,尽快搬开未烧着的衣服物品,检查已燃烧的物品,查看余火是否灭尽。这类火灾隐患较容易控制,只要乘务员严格按要求执行,就能杜绝此类火灾的发生。

(2)油类引起的火灾。从目前掌握的数据来看,这一类火灾主要是由机上烤箱内食物加热时间过长,餐食油脂溢出造成的。这就要求乘务员在使用烤箱时格外留心,在每次启动烤箱时都应检查烤箱内有无上次滞留的食物油渍,在每一次放置食物前,都应用小毛巾擦拭烤箱上遗留下来的异物。了解需加热的温度及烘烤时间,避免食物加热时间过长造成油脂溢出,另外,还应逐一检查加热食物的密封性,以免在飞机起飞和着陆时由于食品密封不牢固造成油脂溢出。这种类型的火灾出现率较高。因此,在使用烤箱烘烤食品时,乘务员应对烤箱进行严密的监控;另外,培训部门要加强对烤箱使用和烤箱失火方面的培训和预案的演练,提高乘务员的处置能力。

(3)电器类或旅客违反规定引起的机上火灾。①电器类火灾。空乘人员要按步骤正确使用飞机上的电器设备,千万不要以粗暴的方式中断电器工作,要让这些电器在完成工作后自动停止。当电器发生火灾时,首先应切断电源,使用海伦灭火瓶灭火。对于像烧水杯的失火类型应拔下水杯,但千万不要将水倒入过热的水杯里。②旅客违反规定引起的机上火灾。卫生间发生火灾主要是由卫生间内的抽水马达自燃和旅客违规吸烟引起的。卫生间失火在飞机火灾中所占的比例较大。根据有关数据统计,45%左右的客舱失火发生在卫生间内。在飞行中,空乘人员应加大"机上禁烟"的广播力度。尤其是在中远程航线上,乘务员可以分时段地进行禁烟广播,警告"瘾君子"旅客在机上绝对禁止吸烟。当卫生间内的烟雾探测器发出警告声,就表明卫生间内存在烟雾或卫生间起火了。乘务员应迅速做出反应,对情况作出判断,以便正确处置。发现违反禁止吸烟规定的旅客,应当立即要求其停止吸烟,并找出烟头丢弃的位置,以免因烟头引起卫生间废纸箱起飞。当卫生间已经发生火灾,最好使用海伦灭火瓶。如果卫生间内无人,乘务员根据门的冷热度来判断是否将门打开进行灭火或者采取门上凿洞灭火的方式。灭火时应注意打开卫生间门时要防止氧气的突然进入加重火情。灭火后,当烟雾从门四周溢出时,应及时用湿毛毯堵住。

(4)可燃性固定物质引起的火灾。旅客所携带物品中夹带的和机上供应品中的干冰等都是引起这类火灾的隐患,这就要求我们加强对旅客行李物品的观察,注意干冰这类物质的正确使用和放置。在这里要重点提出的是当机上发现疑似爆炸物品时的处置方法。由于这类物品会引起大面积火灾,严重危及人机安全,所以在空中遇到这类疑似物品时,首先要报告机长,寻找相关专业人员的帮助,并根据情况采取下列措施:是否要降低高度及降压?是否关闭所有不必要的电源?该物品在专业人员指导下是否可移动?是否用湿物品进行覆盖?是否调整旅客座位?是否组织撤离?

Type of fire

According to the business knowledge and relevant information we have collected and mastered, there are four types of fire in the cabin:

Type A fire caused by paper, cloth and wood; Type B fire caused by oil; Type C caused by electrical appliance class C electrical appliances; Type D fire caused by inflammable fixed substances.

1. The general type of fire caused by paper, wood, cloth. This type of fire usually occurs in cabin seats, cloakrooms, luggage compartments, and especially in winter, when people wear nylon clothes that can spark and ignite under high static pressure. Preventive measures: the theoretical knowledge and safety awareness of flight attendants should be strengthened, so that the flight attendants can strengthen the inspection of flammable space and detect fire in advance. Measure: when this type of fire, flight attendants must quickly take out fire bottle of fire fighting work (i. e. remove the water fire extinguishing bottle), verbal information, tell the nearest flight attendants about the fire according to the response plans division of labor cooperation, move as soon as possible the clothing and items that have not been burnt, check the burning items, check to see if the embers have been destroyed. This type of fire hazard is easier for us to control. As long as the flight attendants strictly follow the requirements, they can prevent the occurrence of such fire.

2. Fire caused by oil. From the data available at present, this kind of fire occurs when the food in the oven is heated for too long time and the grease in the food spilt. The flight attendants should check the oven to see if there is oil stains left before using the oven, and use a small towel to wipe the residue off the oven. They should know the right heating temperature and heating time of the food, and avoid the oil overflow caused by excessive heating of the food. In addition, the sealing of heated food should be checked, so as to avoid the oil overflow due to the insecure sealing during the take-off and landing. The occurrence rate of this type of fire is relatively high, so flight attendants should strictly monitor the oven when heating food; in addition, the training department should enhance the training and exercises on the use of the oven and the oven fire, so as to improve the

handling ability of the flight attendants.

3. Fire caused by electrical appliances or passengers' violation of regulations.

(1) Fire caused by electrical appliances. The cabin crew should use the electrical equipment and facilities correctly and step by step. They should not interrupt their working mode in a rude manner, and wait until the appliance complete their work and stop automatically. When a fire occurs in electrical appliance, the first thing to do is to cut off the power supply, and use Helen fire extinguisher to put out the fire. For the type of fire like the burning water cup, the water cup should be pulled out, but do not pour water into the overheated water cup.

(2) Fire caused by violation of regulations by passengers. Toilet fire is mainly caused by the spontaneous combustion of pumping motor in the toilet and illegal smoking by passengers. Toilet fire accounts for a large proportion of the aircraft fire. According to relevant statistics, about 45% of the cabin fire occurs in the toilet. During the flight, the cabin crew increase the "no-smoking onboard" broadcast. Especially in the mid and long distance flight, flight attendants can broadcast smoking bans by time periods to warn passengers that smoking is absolutely prohibited on the plane. When the smoke detector in the lavatory goes off, it indicates the presence of smoke or a toilet fire. The cabin crew should react quickly and make a judgment on the situation so as to handle it correctly. Passengers who smoke shall be immediately asked to stop smoking and find out where the cigarette butts are left in order to avoid the fire caused by the cigarette butts in the toilet waste carton. When there is a fire in the lavatory, it is best to use the Helen extinguisher. If there is no one in the toilet, the flight attendant will judge whether to open the door to put out the fire or take a hole in the door to put out the fire according to the temperature and heat of the door. When extinguishing the fire, pay attention to prevent the sudden entry of oxygen to aggravate the fire when opening the lavatory door. After extinguishing the fire, when the smoke overflowed from the door, the door should be covered with wet blankets.

4. Fires caused by inflammable fixed substances. The dry ice contained in the items carried by passengers and the dry ice in the supplies on board are all hidden dangers of causing such fires. So this requires us to pay attention to passengers' luggage items and the proper use and storage of substance such as dry ice. What we emphasize is the disposal method when suspected explosives are found on board. Since such items can cause large-scale fires and severely threaten the safety of human and the plane, the first thing to do is to report to the captain and seek the help of relevant professionals, and take the following measures according to the situation: Whether to lower the altitude or to lower the pressure? Should all unnecessary electronic powers be turned off? Can the items be moved under the guidance of professionals? Should it be covered with wet items? Should rearrange passengers' seats? Whether to carry out evacuation, etc.

任务七　灭火后广播

一、常用词汇和表达

extinguish　vt. 熄灭（火）
assign　vt. 分派，选派，分配
explosive　adj. 爆炸的，易爆炸的

二、句型练习

1. We will adjust the seats of passengers near the fire source. Other passengers, please don't walk in the cabin.
我们将调整靠近火源的旅客的座位，其他旅客请不要在机舱内走动。

2. The plane has reached a safe height. You can take off the oxygen mask and breathe normally.
飞机已到达安全高度，您可以摘下氧气面罩，正常呼吸。

3. Don't worry. All our crew members are well trained to deal with such incidents, and the captain is fully capable of landing the aircraft safely.
请不要担心，我们所有的机组人员都接受过良好的训练来处理这类事故，机长完全有能力安全降落飞机。

4. Please sit down, keep calm and obey the cabin crew's command at any time.
请坐下，保持冷静，随时听从乘务员指挥。

5. Please pay attention to the passengers in the upper cabin: your emergency exit is on the left and right side downstairs. There are two standby emergency exits in the upper cabin. Please follow the command of the cabin crew and evacuate from the designated exit.
上舱旅客请注意：您的紧急出口在楼下左右两侧，上舱有两个备用紧急出口，请听从乘务员指挥，从指定出口撤离。

6. Fire has been put out and condition in the cabin is safe. You can take off the oxygen mask and breathe normally.
火已经被扑灭，客舱已经安全。您可以摘下氧气面罩，正常呼吸。

三、对话练习

PAX: Excuse me, Miss. What happened?
旅客：打扰一下，小姐。请问发生了什么事？
CA: There was a small fire in the cabin just now, sir.
乘务员：刚才客舱发生了小的火灾，先生。

PAX:Oh, my God! Is it serious?

旅客:哦,天哪！严重吗？

CA:The fire has been put out. It's all right now. The plane is in good condition.

乘务员:火已经被扑灭了,现在没事了,飞机状态良好。

PAX:Good. Thank you for your hard work.

旅客:那就好,你们辛苦了。

CA:Never mind.

乘务员:没关系。

四、广播词

1

Ladies and gentlemen,

The fire has been completely extinguished. Our aircraft is in good condition and safely cruising as scheduled to _____ Airport. However, we shall be leading the aircraft as soon as possible to carry out further inspection. The estimated arrival time at airport is _____ a. m. /p. m. . We sincerely apologize for any inconvenience. We hope you can understand the reason for making the decision.

Thank you for your cooperation.

女士们、先生们：

火已经完全被扑灭了。我们的飞机状况良好,正在按计划安全驶向_____机场。我们将对飞机做进一步检查。预计到达机场的时间是上午_____/下午_____。给您带来的不便,我们深表歉意。希望您可以理解我们做出这个决定的原因。

谢谢您的配合。

2

Ladies and gentlemen,

The fire has been completely put out. The plane is cruising as scheduled to _____.

Thank you for your assistance and cooperation.

Thank you!

女士们、先生们：

火已经被完全扑灭。飞机将按原计划继续飞往_____。感谢您的协助与合作。

谢谢！

项目小结

特殊情况是飞行过程中受内外多种因素的影响,出现的一系列的意外状况。这些意外状况具有较强的突发性,是人无法预测的。遇到这种意外状况时,旅客会出现不同程度的慌张、紧张、焦急等情绪,因此需要空中乘务人员对飞行过程中遇到的突发状况作出积极、正确的回应,在播报过程中应保证语言简洁、逻辑清晰、语气平和。如果空中乘务人员缺乏规范播报的能力,客舱广播不仅无法发挥其应有的作用,反而会给旅客带来一定的负面影响。

项目训练

1. 在飞往北京的航班上,一名旅客突然出现了口吐白沫的症状,假如你是乘务员,应如何对旅客进行客舱安全广播?

2. 根据客舱内突然失火的情况,小组拟写广播词,模仿乘务员和不同旅客。每个小组在模拟时,其他小组要认真观看,并做好记录。然后根据民航广播播音用语的基本要求进行自我评价,并与其他小组进行互评。

项 目	考核要点	完成情况	评定等级
客舱广播	播报及时		
	播报语气适当		
	广播词格式符合规范		
	广播词表达准确		
	语音音量适中		
	语调生动		
综合评定等级			

项目七　介绍性广播

项目目标

知识目标
了解常见的介绍性广播词的内涵和用途；
掌握介绍性广播词的核心要素和基本词汇表达；
熟悉相关的介绍性广播词。

能力目标
通过对介绍性广播词理论知识的学习，端正服务态度，培养民航服务意识，做好对客服务的心理准备、思想准备和行为准备。

素质目标
掌握介绍性广播词的语言规范要求，提高自身职业素养。

知识框架

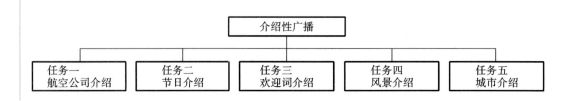

任务一　航空公司介绍

China Southern Airlines

China Southern Airlines was established on February 1, 1991. Since then, it acquired and merged with a number of domestic airlines, becoming one of China's "Big Three" airlines(alongside Air China and China Eastern Airlines). With flight operations based at Guangzhou award-winning Baiyun International Airport, China Southern Airlines' company logo can be seen around the globe with brilliant red kapok delicately adoring a blue vertical tail.

The airline owns and operates its own independent training centers for pilots and flight attendants. China Southern Airlines, with more than 3 300 comprehensively trained and experienced pilots, is the only Chinese carrier that has an independent capability of "building its pilots from the ground up". The Flight Training Center which is a joint venture with CAE(the world's leading manufacturer of flight simulators) is the Asia's largest flight training center. The Airline enjoys a strong aircraft maintenance capability through its joint-venture company Guangzhou Aircraft Maintenance & Engineering Co., Ltd. (GAMECO for short), which has built Asia's largest aircraft maintenance hangar. The Airline has 20 branches in China. In 2012, China Southern Airlines carried 86.5 million domestic and international passengers with an average load factor of 81%.

China Southern Airlines is the largest airline in China, measured in terms of fleet size as well as the number of passengers carried, and is also the first in Asia in terms of fleet size. The airline currently serves destinations to 841 cities in 162 countries. It has developed an extensive network to Southeast Asia and also has become the Chinese airline with the largest presence in Australia. It is also considering expanding into the South American market, as well as further expansion into the African market.

In 1995, 2001, 2003, 2004 and 2007, China Southern Airlines was honored the "Golden Roc Cup", which is the most prestigious safe flight operation award in the Chinese aviation industry, becoming the only Chinese carrier maintaining and the longest safety flying record and occupying a leading position in the international aviation industry.

(资料来源:http://en.wikipedia.org/wiki/China_Southern_Airlines。)

中国南方航空公司

中国南方航空公司成立于1991年2月1日。当时,它收购和兼并了多家国内航空公司,成为中国航空的"三巨头"之一(另外两家是中国国际航空公司和中国东方航空公司)。南航总部设于屡获殊荣的广州白云国际机场,其公司航徽是蓝色垂直尾翼镶红色木棉花。

南航拥有自己独立的飞行员和乘务员培训中心。南航飞行实力出众,拥有超过3 300名训练有素、经验丰富的飞行员,是目前国内唯一一家拥有独立培养飞行员能力的航空公司。与全球知名飞行模拟器制造商CAE合资建立的飞行训练中心是亚洲规模最大的飞行训练中心。南航拥有雄厚的机务维修能力,旗下合资公司广州飞机维修工程有限公司(GAMECO)建有亚洲最大的飞机维修机库。南航拥有20家分公司。2012年,南航承运国内国际旅客人次达86 500 000,平均客座率达81%。

南航是中国机队规模最大、载客人数最多的航空公司,也是亚洲机队规模最大的航空公司。南航目前的航线涵盖了162个国家在内的841个城市。公司已建立了庞大的东南亚航线网络,同时,南航也是中国在澳大利亚规模最大的航空公司。目前南航正考虑进一步拓展南美和非洲市场。

在1995、2001、2003、2004、2007年,南航五度夺得中国民航年度安全最高奖"金鹏杯",成为国内安全星级最高、安全飞行记录最长的航空公司,在国际上也处于领先地位。

Air China

Air China Limited ("Air China") and its predecessor, the former Air China, were founded in 1988. Air China is China's exclusive national flag carrier for civil aviation, a member of the Star Alliance, the world's largest airline alliance. In addition to leading ahead of its domestic competitors in passenger and freight air transport and related services, it also provides special flight services for China's leaders on official visits to other countries.

Air China's logo consists of an artistic phoenix pattern, the Chinese name of the airline written in calligraphy by former Chinese leader Mr. Deng Xiaoping, and "AIR CHINA" written in English. The phoenix logo is also an artistic transfiguration of the word "VIP". The color is the traditional Chinese red which implies auspiciousness, completion, peace and happiness, and expresses Air China's sincere passion to serve society and endless pursuit of safety. Air China holds its vision and orientation as "a well-established global airline", the connotation of which is to realize four strategic objectives: leading competitiveness in the world market, continuously enhanced development potential, excellent and distinguished travel experiences for passengers, and steadily increasing profits. Its enterprise spirit emphasizes "serving the world with a warm heart and guiding the future by innovation". Its enterprise mission is to "meet the requirements of customers and create mutual value". Its enterprise sense of worth is to "deliver a high level of service and earn universal approval from the pubic". Its service philosophy is "Credibility, Convenience, Comfort and Choice".

As of December 31, 2020, Air China (including its holding companies) owns a total of 707 aircrafts, featuring Boeing and Airbus, with an average lifespan of 7.74 years. It operates 674 passenger routes. In collaboration with other Star Alliance member airlines, its service network is further extended to 1 300 destinations in 195 countries.

Air China's frequent flyer program "Phoenix Miles", has the longest history of any frequent flyer program in China. Through the integration of its various memberships under Air China's holding companies and joint-stock companies, all are unified as "Phoenix Miles". As of December 2020, the Phoenix Miles program had more than 68.176 million members. For seven consecutive years from 2007 to 2013, Air China was listed among the "Top 500 global brands", becoming the only civil aviation airline ever listed.

（资料来源：http://www.airchina.com.cn/en/about_us/company.shtml。）

中国国际航空公司

中国国际航空股份有限公司（简称"国航"），其前身为中国国际航空公司，成立于1988年。国航是中国唯一挂载国旗飞行的民用航空公司和世界最大的航空联盟——星空联盟成员。它承担着中国国家领导人出访的专机任务；在航空客运、货运及相关服务方面，均处于国内领先地位。

国航的企业标识由一只艺术化的凤凰和邓小平同志书写的"中国国际航空公司"以及英文"AIR CHINA"构成。国航标志是凤凰，同时又是英文"VIP"的艺术形式，颜色为中国传统的大红,具有吉祥、圆满、祥和、幸福的寓意,寄予着国航人服务社会的真挚情怀和对安全事业的永恒追求。国航的愿景和定位是"具有国际知名度的航空公司";其内涵是实现"竞争实力世界前列、发展能力持续增强、客户体验美好独特、相关利益稳步提升"的四大战略目标;企业精神强调"爱心服务世界,创新导航未来";企业使命是"满足顾客需求,创造共有价值";企业价值观是"服务至高境界,公众普遍认同";服务理念是"放心、顺心、舒心、动心"。

截至 2020 年 12 月 31 日,国航(含控股公司)共拥有以波音、空中客车为主的各型飞机 707 架,平均机龄 7.74 年。经营客运航线已达 674 条。通过与星空联盟成员等航空公司合作,国航将服务进一步拓展到 195 个国家的 1 300 个目的地。

国航拥有中国历史最长的常旅客计划"凤凰知音",又通过整合控股,将参股公司旅客会员统纳入"凤凰知音"品牌。截至 2020 年 12 月,"凤凰知音"会员已达到 6 817.6 万人。2007 年至 2013 年,国航连续七年入选"世界品牌 500 强",成为中国民航唯一一家进入"世界品牌 500 强"的企业。

China Eastern Airlines

China Eastern Airlines Corporation Limited was founded in April 1995, with its headquarter in Shanghai. It ranks second among the three largest airlines in China in terms of passengers carried, next only to China Southern Airlines. Besides, China Eastern Airlines administers 11 branches including the Northwest, Yunnan, Shandong, Shanxi, Anhui, Jiangxi, Hebei, Zhejiang, Gansu and Beijing.

China Eastern and its subsidiary Shanghai Airlines became the 14th member of Sky Team on June 21, 2011. With its main hub in Shanghai near the Yangtze River Delta Area, China Eastern Airlines' network connects over 150 destinations, including most of the major cities in China and many international destinations in Asia, Europe, Australia, and the US. In 2012, China Eastern Airlines carried 73.08 million domestic and international passengers with an average load factor of 73%.

China Eastern Airlines' logo is a white artistic swallow on a circle background comprised of a red semicircle resembling the sun and a dark blue semicircle resembling the sea. The tail of the swallow is also a transfiguration of the word "CE", short for "China Eastern".

China Eastern Airlines's frequent flyer program is called Eastern Miles. Enrollment is free of charge. Eastern Miles members can earn miles on flights as well as through consumption with China Eastern's credit card. When enough miles are collected, members can be upgraded to VIP. VIP membership of Eastern Miles can be divided into two types: Golden Card membership and Silver Card membership. VIP membership can enjoy extra privileged services.

China Eastern Airlines was the first civilian airline listed on the New York Stock Exchange, the Shanghai Stock Exchange, and the Hong Kong Stock Exchange. With a brand value reaching RMB 21 758 000 000, it ranks 42nd on the list of China's 500 Most Influential Brands, as announced by World Brand Value Lab 2010. In 2012, China Eastern was awarded the "Golden Ting Award" at the China Capital Market Annual Conference

2012, recognizing it as one of the 50 most valuable Chinese brands by WPP and ranking in the top 10 of *Fortune* China's CSR Ranking in 2013.

（资料来源：http://www.chinahighlights.com/china-airline/eastern-airlines.htm；http://en.wikipedia.org/wiki/China_Eastern_Airlines。）

中国东方航空公司

中国东方航空股份有限公司成立于1995年4月，总部设在上海，它是中国三大航空公司之一，载客量仅次于中国南方航空。此外，东航下辖有11家分公司，包括西北、云南、山东、山西、安徽、江西、河北、浙江、甘肃、北京。

东航及其子公司上海航空于2011年6月21日成为天合联盟的第14个成员。东航的枢纽机场位于长江三角洲地区的上海，其航线网络覆盖了150多个城市，包括了中国各主要城市以及亚洲、欧洲、澳大利亚和美国的主要城市。2012年，东航国内及国际载客量达7 308万人次，平均客座率为73%。

东航的航徽基本构图为圆形，取红蓝白三色，以寓意太阳、大海的上下半圆与燕子的组合，表现东航的企业形象。燕子尾部的线条勾勒出东航英文名"China Eastern"的首字母CE两字。

东航常旅客计划名为"东方万里行"。会员注册免费。会员可通过乘坐东航航班和消费东航信用卡两种方式累积里程。里程累积到一定限度后，会员可升级为VIP。"东方万里行"VIP会员分为两种：金卡会员和银卡会员。VIP会员可享受额外的特权服务。

东航是在纽约证券交易所、上海证券交易所和香港联合交易所上市的第一家民用航空公司。根据2010年世界品牌价值实验室公布的数据，东航品牌价值达217.58亿人民币，荣登"中国最具影响力500强品牌榜"第42名。2012年东航被全球品牌传播机构WPP评为"最具价值中国品牌50强"，获评第八届中国证券市场年会最高奖项"金鼎奖"，并入选《财富》杂志（中文版）2013年中国企业社会责任排行榜前十强。

Singapore Airlines

Singapore Airlines Limited (SIA) is the flag carrier of Singapore and a 5-star airline. Singapore Airlines operates a hub at Changi Airport and has a strong presence in the Southeast Asia, East Asia, South Asia, and "Kangaroo Route" markets. It is also the launch customer of Airbus A380, currently the world's largest passenger aircraft.

Singapore Airlines maintains a modern fleet of 103 aircraft. As of July 1, 2014, the average age of our fleet stands at six years and 11 months. It means that it is one of the world's youngest and most fuel efficient airlines. The Singapore Airlines Group has over 20 subsidiaries, covering a range of airline-related services from cargo to engine overhaul. The Singapore Airlines Group will continue to invest in related businesses, rather than seek to diversify outside of the aviation industry.

In 2004, SIA began non-stop trans-Pacific flights from Singapore to Los Angeles and New York, utilizing the Airbus A340-500. These flights marked the first non-stop air services between Singapore and the USA. The Singapore to New York flight held the record for the longest scheduled commercial flight, with a flying time of about 18 hours each way. It ranks among the top 15 carriers worldwide in terms of revenue passenger kilometers, and 10th in the world for international passengers carried. On December 15, 2010, Singapore Airlines was announced by the International Air Transport Association as the second largest airline in the world by market capitalization with a worth of 14 billion US dollars, SIA once had a 49% shareholding in Virgin Atlantic before selling it to Delta Air Lines for $277 million in December 2012.

Branding and publicity efforts have revolved primarily around flight crew, in contrast to most other airlines, who tend to emphasize aircraft and services in general. In particular, the promotion of its female flight attendants, known as Singapore Girls has been widely successful and is a common feature in most of the airline's advertisements and publications. This branding strategy aims to build a mythical aura around the Singapore Girls, and portray her as representative of Asian hospitality and grace.

Singapore Airlines' frequent flyer program has two categories: Kris Flyer and The Priority Passenger Service(PPS)Club. As a member, passengers can earn Kris Flyer miles when they fly on Singapore Airlines, Silk Air or any of Singapore airlines' partners, which include airlines in the Star Alliance network. Priority Passenger Service (PPS) is for passengers who have accumulated a PPS Value of S$25 000 within a period of 12 consecutive months.

新加坡航空公司

新加坡航空公司（新航）是新加坡的国家航空公司，同时也是一家五星级航空公司。新航以樟宜机场为基地，在东南亚、东亚和南亚拥有强大的航线网络，并占据"袋鼠航线"的一部分市场。新航还是首个营运全球最大客机 A380 的航空公司。

新航目前拥有由 103 架飞机组成的现代化机群。截至 2014 年 7 月 1 日，机队的平均服役年龄为 6 年 11 个月，这意味着新航是世界上机队服役时间最短、燃油效率使用最高的航空公司之一。新加坡航空集团拥有 20 家子公司，其业务覆盖了从货运到发动机维修等一系列的航空相关服务。未来该公司将继续投资与行业相关的业务，而不是寻求航空业之外的多元化发展。

2004 年，新航推出了跨太平洋航班，以 A340-500 来营运的全球最长的直航航班：新加坡—洛杉矶和新加坡—纽约。这是新加坡和美国之间的首趟直航航班。其中，新加坡—纽约的航班更是创造了商业航班的最长飞行记录：单程飞行时间达 18 小时。若以人均千米收入计算，新航是全球十五大航空公司之一；若以国际航线载客量计算，新航是全球第十大航空公司。2010 年 12 月 15 日，国际航空运输协会宣布，新加坡航空公司以市值 140 亿美元，荣膺全球第二大航空公司。2012 年 12 月，新航将持有的维珍大西洋航空公司 49% 的股权，以 2.77 亿美元的价格，出售给达美航空公司。

与其他大多数公司强调其飞机和整体服务不同的是，新航在品牌推广及宣传工作上是紧紧围绕机组人员进行宣传的。尤其是对新航空姐（人们常称其为"新加坡女孩"）的宣传，获得了广泛的成功。新航空姐已被打造成该公司营销的一张名片，该品牌战略的目的是围绕新航空姐，打造一个神话般的光环，将其定位为亚洲人民热情与优雅的化身。

新航的常旅客计划分为两种：新航奖励计划（Kris Flyer）和新航礼遇嘉宾俱乐部（PPS Club）。旅客注册成新航会员之后，在乘坐新航航班、胜安航班或新航合作伙伴的航班（包括星空联盟网络的航班）时，就可以累积 Kris Flyer 里程数。PPS Club 是针对连续 12 个月内累积的 PPS 值达到 25 000 新元的旅客推出的会员服务。

Cathay Pacific Airways

Cathay Pacific is the home airline of Hong Kong, with its head office and main hub located at Hong Kong International Airport. It is a founding member of the Oneworld alliance, with its subsidiary, DragonAir, as an affiliate member. It's one of the world's most modern wide-body fleets, with some 90 new aircrafts currently on order at an aggregate list price of about HK＄220 billion.

Its extensive worldwide network offers connections to almost 190 destinations in 47 countries and territories.

Cathay Pacific Airways has recently been named "World's Best Airline" in the annual Skytrax World Airline Awards, 2014. This is the fourth time Cathay Pacific has received the World's Best Airline honor—the only airline to achieve such a feat. The carrier also took the title in 2003, 2005 and 2009. Skytrax is acknowledged as running one of the most comprehensive customer satisfaction surveys in the airline industry. Airline passengers from more than 160 countries participated in the latest survey, which covered 245 airlines worldwide. The survey measures standards across 41 key performance indicators of airline products and services.

Cathay Pacific is a partner of Asia Miles, Asia's leading travel reward program. Asia Miles has over 500 partners in nine categories, including 21 airline partners, and more than 6 million members. Members can earn Asia Miles to over 1 000 destinations worldwide.

Cathay Pacific has been the home airline of Hong Kong for close to 70 years and it is deeply committed to building the city into one of the world's great aviation hubs. The airline does this through its huge investment in new aircraft, its world beating seats, lounges and other products, its renowned service straight from the heart and an ever-expanding network of destinations. In addition to making a major contribution to Hong Kong's economy through its investments in education and infrastructure, Cathay Pacific is also actively involved in a variety of community initiatives under its Corporate Social Responsibility(CSR) banner.

Based on data for 2012, Cathay Pacific currently ranks as the world's 19th largest airline in the world by operating revenue. It ranks 14th largest in the world in terms of revenue passenger kilometer.

（资料来源：http://www.cathaypacific.com/cx/sc_CN.html。）

国 泰 航 空

国泰航空是一家香港航空公司，其总部和枢纽机场位于香港国际机场。它是创办"寰宇一家"联盟的成员航空公司之一，其附属公司港龙航空亦为"寰宇一家"的附属会员。该公司是全球最现代化的宽体机队之一，目前订购中的新飞机约90架，总标价约2 200亿港元。

其环球航线网络连接了47个国家及地区，服务近190个航点。

国泰在2014年Skytrax世界航空公司大奖评选中，再度当选为"全球最佳航空公司"，成为全球唯一四度夺得此殊荣的航空公司。此前，国泰先后于2003年、2005年及2009年荣膺该荣誉称号。Skytrax此项就旅客满意度的评选，被誉为航空界最全面的调查之一。参与调查的旅客来自超过160个国家，涵盖全球245家航空公司，调查对41项有关航空产品及服务的主要表现指标进行评级。

国泰是"亚洲万里通"常旅客计划的伙伴航空公司之一。"亚洲万里通"现拥有超过500个、分属9个类别的合作伙伴,包括21家伙伴航空公司,会员人数逾600万。会员可累积"亚洲万里通"里程数,用以兑换前往全球1 000多个城市和地区的机票。

国泰以香港为家近70年,一直坚守承诺,致力于将香港打造成为世界级航空枢纽。该公司大量投资,想要通过引入新机型、首屈一指的客舱座位、机场贵宾室和其他产品、享誉盛名的"发自内心的服务",以及不断拓展的航线网络实现这个目标。此外,在投资教育和基础设施,推动香港经济发展的同时,国泰也积极响应企业社会责任(CSR),参与了多项社区活动。

截至2012年,若以营运收益计算,国泰为全球第19大航空公司;若以旅客周转量计算,国泰航空是全球第14大航空公司。

Juneyao Airlines Co., Ltd

Juneyao Airlines Co., Ltd (hereinafter referred to as Juneyao Airlines) is an emerging private Airlines based in Shanghai established by Juneyao Group. Shanghai Juneyao (Group) Co., Ltd and Shanghai Juneyao Airlines Investment Co., Ltd., jointly set up the private capital Airlines, in May 2015, listed in A share market.

Main base: Shanghai Hongqiao International Airport, Shanghai Pudong International Airport. Juneyao Airlines has signed a memorandum with Airbus to introduce its A320 family. Juneyao Airlines plans to take Shanghai as the center and form the route network layout with domestic and surrounding regional routes as the hub network. A route network has been formed, with Shanghai Hongqiao International Airport and Shanghai Pudong International Airport as the major hubs home and abroad. In 2010, a route network has gradually taken shape, connecting transit routes in cities around Shanghai and radiating the whole country. International air routes from Shanghai will be opened in stages.

Second base: Nanjing Lukou International Airport

On May 15, 2018, Juneyao Airlines won the first place in the "Outstanding Flight Attendant Team in China" ranking. In December 2018, Jixiang Aviation delivered the second Boeing 787, and painted China Silk Road coating.

Juneyao Airlines received its sixth 787-9 Dreamliner on November 20, 2019.

In October 2020, it was awarded the title of the National Transportation System Advanced Group to combat COVID-19.

Juneyao Jixiang Airlines will be in accordance with the "Safety, Punctuality, Delicate service" business philosophy, expand the route network and transport scale, improve the quality of service, committed to becoming an excellent international airline.

上海吉祥航空有限公司(简称:吉祥航空或Juneyao Airlines)是国内著名民营企业均瑶集团成立的以上海为基地的新兴民营航空公司,是由均瑶集团所属的上海均瑶(集团)有限公司和上海均瑶航空投资有限公司共同投资筹建的民营资本航空公司,已于2015年5月在A股上市。

主营基地:上海虹桥国际机场、上海浦东国际机场。吉祥航空同空客公司签订了引进空客A320系列的备忘录。吉祥航空规划以上海为中心,形成以国内和周边地区航线为枢纽网络的航线网络布局。形成以上海虹桥国际机场和上海浦东国际机场为主要枢纽的国内外航线网络,2010年逐步形成以上海周边城市中转连程并辐射全国的航线网络。分阶段开通从上海出发的国际航线。

第二基地:南京禄口国际机场

2018年5月15日,吉祥航空获得"中国优秀空乘团队"排行榜的第一名。2018年12月,吉祥航空第二架波音787飞机交付使用,彩绘中国丝路涂装。

2019年11月20日,吉祥航空接收了第六架787-9梦想飞机。

2020年10月,吉祥航空被评为"全国交通运输系统抗击新冠肺炎疫情先进集体"。

上海吉祥航空将按照"安全、准点、精致服务"的经营理念,快速扩大航线网络和运输规模,提高服务质量,致力于成为一家卓越的国际化航空公司。

China Southwest Airlines

China Southwest Airlines(SZ/CXN) was established on October 15,1987. It is the first backbone air transportation enterprise established in accordance with the principle of separating government from enterprise approved by the State Council. It operates 156 domestic routes and 11 international and regional routes to more than 60 cities. In 1998, a total turnover of 610 million ton km, 4.75 million passengers and 100 000 tons of cargo and mail transportation were completed. According to the civil aviation reform and reorganization strategy of China in 2002, Air China is the main body, together with China National Aviation Corporation, Southwest Airlines and other enterprises to establish China Aviation Group Corporation.

"Safety first, Normal flight and High quality service" are the leading policies of the company. The Southwest Branch of Air China has a flying team with excellent style and excellent technology. Among the company's pilots, more than 180 have won the "Flight Safety Merit Award" and "Flight Safety Gold Medal" issued by CAAC, ranking first in China's civil aviation industry. The company has maintained the safe flight record of Chengdu-Lhasa route, which is the most difficult flight in the world, and successfully opened the route from Chengdu to Qamdo Bangda Airport, the highest civil airport in the world. In 1996 and 2000, the company won the "Golden Roc Cup", the highest award of safety flight in China's civil aviation industry. Southwest Branch of Air China pays attention to the construction of service quality, and both air service and ground service maintain a high level. In November 2001, the Southwest Branch of Air China passed the certifcation of ISO10012-1 measurement and testing system organized by the General Administration of Quality Supervision, Inspection and Quarantine of the People's Republic of China.

中国西南航空公司

中国西南航空公司(SZ/CXN)成立于1987年10月15日,是国务院批准的我国第一家按政企分开原则建立起来的骨干航空运输企业。经营着156条国内航线和11条国际和地区航线,通往60多个城市。1998年完成总周转量6.1亿吨公里,旅客运输量475万人,货邮运输量10万吨。根据2002年中国民航改革重组战略,以中国国际航空公司为主体,联合中国航空总公司和中国西南航空公司等企业,共同组建中国航空集团公司。

"安全第一、正常飞行、优质服务"是公司经营的主导方针。中国国际航空公司西南分公司拥有作风优良、技术过硬的飞行队伍。公司的飞行员中,先后有180余人荣获中国民用航空局颁发的"飞行安全功勋奖"和"飞行安全金质奖章",位居全国民航业第一。公司保持了世界上飞行难度最大的成都—拉萨航线的安全飞行纪录,成功地开辟了成都通往世界海拔最高的民用机场昌都邦达机场的航线。1996年和2000年,公司两度荣获中国民航航空安全最高奖"金鹏杯"。中国国际航空公司西南分公司注重服务质量建设,空中服务和地面服务都保持了较高水平。2001年11月,中国国际航空公司西南分公司通过了国家质量监督检验检疫总局组织的ISO10012-1计量检测体系的认证。

任务二 节日介绍

在节假日广播时,语气要热情,要让旅客感受到浓浓的节日气氛。

一、新年欢迎词

女士们、先生们:

新年好!我代表全体机组人员欢迎您乘坐_____航空公司的_____航班前往_____(中途降落_____)。今天是新年的第一天,我代表全体机组人员向您送上一份最真挚的祝福,期盼您的每一天都有幸福的陪伴。让我们在这喜庆的氛围中共度这一美好时刻,衷心地祝您在新的一年里身体健康、万事如意。

女士们、先生们,飞机很快就要起飞了,请您坐好,系好安全带,并把小桌板和座椅靠背调整到正常位置。

本次航班共有4位乘务员,您可以随时呼叫我们,我们将十分乐意为您提供及时周到的服务。祝您旅途愉快!谢谢!

Ladies and gentlemen,

Happy New Year! On behalf of all the crew, I would like to welcome you aboard _____ Airlines' flight _____ for _____ (via _____). Today is the first day of the new year, on behalf of all the crew, I send you the most sincere wishes. Let us share this wonderful moment in this festive atmosphere. I sincerely wish you good health and all the best in the new year.

Ladies and gentlemen, the plane will take off soon. Please sit down, fasten your seat belt and adjust the small table board and seat back to the normal position.

There are four flight attendants on this flight. Please call us at any time. We will be happy to provide you timely and thoughtful service. Wish you a pleasant journey! Thank you!

☆Replace the blanks with:
Sichuan/3U8998/Chengdu/Changsha

Air China/CA176/Beijing/Shanghai

China Eastern/MU2527/Dalian/Qingdao

二、元宵节

女士们、先生们：

早上好/下午好/晚上好！今天是元宵佳节，我们很高兴在这浓浓的节日气氛中为您提供服务。元宵节是我国的传统佳节，元宵节的传统食物是元宵。本次航班的机组人员也为大家准备了元宵，希望这香甜的元宵能带给您一份轻松和温馨。稍后供应时，我们将广播通知您，最后祝您旅途愉快！

谢谢！

Good morning/afternoon/evening, ladies and gentlemen,

We are glad to be at your service on the traditional Lantern Festival. The tradition food of the festival is Yuanxiao. Our flight crew has prepared Yuanxiao. We hope it will bring you ease and warmth on this special day. We will broadcast when it is available. Wish you a pleasant journey!

Thank you!

☆ **Words and expressions**：

lantern ['læntən] n. 灯笼

Lantern Festival 元宵节

三、端午节

女士们、先生们：

早上好/下午好/晚上好！今天是我国的传统佳节端午节。相传端午节是为了纪念爱国诗人屈原，到今天已经有两千多年的历史了。在这一天，我国各地都有很多的民俗活动，最有代表性的活动就是赛龙舟和吃粽子。本次航班的机组人员为大家准备了粽子，希望能带给您一份轻松和温馨。稍后供应时，我们将广播通知您，祝您旅途愉快！

谢谢！

Good morning/afternoon/evening, ladies and gentlemen,

Today is the traditional Dragon Boat Festival of China, which is to commemorate the great poet of China Qu Yuan. It has a history of two thousand years. The most representative activities of the festival is dragon boat racing and eating Zongzi. We have prepared Zongzi. We hope it will bring you ease and warmth. We will broadcast when it is available. Wish you a pleasant journey!

Thank you!

☆ **Words and expressions**：

commemorate [kə'meməreɪt] vt. 纪念

四、国庆节

女士们、先生们：

早上好/下午好/晚上好！今天是我们伟大祖国的生日，在这里，让我们一起祝福我们的祖国更加繁荣昌盛。

在这段旅途中，我们为您准备了点心/早点/午餐/晚餐及各种冷热饮，供应时，我们将广播通知您。

祝您旅途愉快！

Good morning/afternoon/evening, ladies and gentlemen,

Today is the National Day holiday of China. We hope our motherland will have a brighter future.

We have prepared snacks/refreshment/lunch/dinner with beverages. We will make announcement when they are available.

Wish you a pleasant journey!

五、中秋节

女士们、先生们：

早上好/下午好/晚上好！今天是农历的八月十五，是我国传统的中秋佳节，在这里，我代表全体机组成员向您说一声节日快乐！中秋节是我国的一个古老节日，人们在这一天有吃月饼的习俗，本次航班也为各位旅客准备了月饼，希望能给您的旅途带来一份轻松和温馨。祝您旅途愉快！

谢谢！

Good morning/afternoon/evening, ladies and gentlemen,

Today is August 15 in lunar calendar, the Mid-autumn Festival of China. On behalf of all the crew members, we would like to say to you "Happy Mid-autumn Festival". We have prepared moon cakes for all passengers. We hope it will bring you ease and warmth. Wish you a pleasant journey!

Thank you!

任务三　欢迎词介绍

一、专机欢迎词

尊敬的_____主席及贵宾们：

你们好！首先我代表全体机组人员热烈欢迎您乘坐_____航空公司的专机前往

_____（中途降落_____）。能为您提供服务我们感到非常荣幸。飞机很快就要起飞了，请您坐好，系好安全带，并把小桌板和座椅靠背调整到正常位置。

如果您有需要，请您随时呼叫，我们十分乐意为您提供及时周到的服务。

预祝各位旅客旅途愉快！

谢谢！

Good morning/afternoon/evening, your Excellency/President/Distinguished guests,

The captain and the crew are pleased to welcome you aboard _____ Airlines' flight to _____ (via _____), and we are honored to be at your service.

We will be taking off shortly. Please be sure that your seat belt is fastened, your tray is in upright position.

If there is anything we can do for you, please call us at any time. We will be happy to provide you timely and thoughtful service.

Wish you a pleasant journey!

☆Replace the blanks with：

Xiamen/Chengdu/Jinan

China Southern/Shenyang/Xi'an

China Southern/Sanya/Hangzhou

二、各国使节欢迎词

尊敬的各国使节：

早上好/下午好/晚上好！我代表全体机组人员热烈欢迎您乘坐中国_____航空公司的班机前往_____（中途降落_____）。能为您提供服务我们感到非常荣幸。

飞机很快就要起飞了，请您坐好，系好安全带，并把小桌板和座椅靠背调整到正常位置。

如果您有需要，请您随时呼叫，我们十分乐意为您提供及时周到的服务。

预祝各位旅客旅途愉快！谢谢！

Good morning/afternoon/evening, ambassadors,

The captain and your crew welcome you aboard _____ Airlines' flight to _____ (via _____), and we are honored to be at your service.

We will be taking off shortly. Please be sure that your seat belt is fastened, your tray table and seat back is in upright position.

If there is anything we can do for you, please call us at any time. We will be happy to provide you timely and thoughtful service.

Wish you a pleasant journey!

☆Replace the blanks with：

Air China/Lasa/Chengdu

Shandong/Urumqi/Xi'an

三、劳务专家欢迎词

尊敬的各位劳务专家：

早上好/下午好/晚上好！

欢迎您乘坐_____航空公司的班机前往_____（中途降落_____）。我代表全体机组人员向所有专家表示最亲切的问候。我们非常荣幸为您服务。

飞机很快就要起飞了，请您坐好，系好安全带，并把小桌板和座椅靠背调整到正常位置。

本次航班共有_____位乘务员，您可以随时呼叫我们，我们十分乐意为您提供及时周到的服务。

预祝各位旅客旅途愉快！谢谢！

Good morning/afternoon/evening, your honoured experts,

The captain and your crew sincerely welcome you aboard _____ Airlines' flight to _____ (via _____). We would like to extend our warmest greetings to all the experts on board and we are honored to be at your service.

We will be taking off shortly. Please be sure that your seat belt is fastened and your tray table is in upright position.

There are _____ attendants on this flight. If there is anything we can do for you, please call us at any time. We will be happy to provide you timely and thoughtful service.

Wish you a pleasant journey!

☆Replace the blanks with：

Xiamen/Chengdu/Jinan/6

China Southern/Shenyang/Xi'an/6

China Southern/Sanya/Hangzhou/6

四、专机落地后广播

尊敬的首相阁下，尊敬的代表团贵宾们，女士们、先生们：

本架飞机已经降落在_____国际机场，外面温度为_____摄氏度。等飞机完全停稳后，请您再解开安全带，带好全部手提物品准备下飞机。

在这段旅途中，对您给予我们工作上的协助，我们表示衷心感谢，并期待再次为您服务！最后，祝您访问成功！

谢谢！

Your Prime Minister/Premier and all other members of the delegation, ladies and gentlemen,

Our plane has just landed at _____ Airport. The outside temperature is _____ degrees Celsius. Please unfasten your seat belt and take all your belongings for disembarking after the plane stops completely.

Thank you for your assistance during the flight. We look forward to serving you next time and we wish you a successful visit!

Thank you!

☆**Words and expressions**：

delegation ［ˌdelɪ'geɪʃn］ n. 代表团

☆**Replace the blanks with**：

Beijing Capital International/32
Shanghai Pudong International/9
Guangzhou Baiyun/18
Sanya Fenghuang/30

任务四　风景介绍

　　飞机在飞行途中会飞越很多风景名胜,乘务员要时常担任导游的角色,让航程中的旅客感受到山水与人文景观之美。本节列举了部分风景简介,乘务员要通过以下练习,做好介绍工作,要让旅客有身临其境的感觉。一篇优秀的风景介绍词必须有丰富的内容做支撑,同时,也要将语言表达技巧和具体的内容融会贯通。大家可以将下列内容作为参考,进行表达练习。

一、万里长城

　　万里长城是我国古代的军事建筑工程,同时,它也是中华民族的象征,被誉为世界建筑史上的奇迹。对中国人来说,长城是意志、勇气和力量的标志,象征着中华民族伟大的力量。今天的长城成为连接中国人民和世界人民友谊的桥梁,是世界著名的游览胜地。

The Great Wall

　　The Great Wall was a military architecture in ancient China. It has now become a symbol of Chinese nation and witnessed its immense pride. It is regarded as a miracle in the architectural history of the world. For Chinese people, the Great Wall is a symbol of perseverance, courage and power, resembling the greatness of Chinese nation. Today, it has become a bridge that connects Chinese people and the world's well-known tourism resort.

architecture ［'ɑ:kɪtektʃə］ n. 建筑
immense ［ɪ'mens］ adj. 巨大的,广大的
resemble ［rɪ'zembl］ v. 像,类似于

二、颐和园

　　颐和园是清代的皇家园林,前身为清漪园,坐落在北京西郊,占地约290公顷,与北京大学、清华大学相邻,是国家重点旅游景点。标志性建筑有昆明湖、万寿山、长廊、十七孔桥

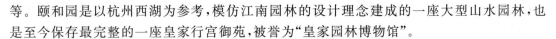

等。颐和园是以杭州西湖为参考，模仿江南园林的设计理念建成的一座大型山水园林，也是至今保存最完整的一座皇家行宫御苑，被誉为"皇家园林博物馆"。

The Summer Place

The Summer Palace was a royal garden of Qing Dynasty, originally named Qingyi Garden. It is located in the northwestern suburbs of Beijing. Occupying an area of about 290 hectares, and adjacent to Peking University and Tsinghua University, it is one of the key national tourist resorts. The landmark architectures include Kunming Lake, the Longevity Hill, the Long Corridor, and the 17-Arc Bridge. The Summer Palace was constructed with reference to the West Lake of Hangzhou and borrowed the ideas of South China gardens. It is also the best preserved royal palace in China. The Summer Palace is regarded as "the museum of royal gardens".

adjacent   [əˈdʒeɪsnt]   adj. 邻近的
resort   [rɪˈzɔːrt]   n. 度假胜地
preserve   [prɪˈzɜːrv]   v. 保护，保存

三、五台山

五台山位于山西省东北部五台县境内，因五座山峰如五根擎天的大柱子，拔地而起，峰顶又平坦如台，故名五台山。五台山由五座山峰环抱而成，风光秀美，气候凉爽，是避暑胜地。五台山的佛光寺和南禅寺是中国现存最早的两座木结构建筑。五台山位居中国四大佛教名山之首，它以源远流长的佛教文化和古建筑群闻名于世。1982年五台山风景名胜区被国务院列为第一批国家级风景名胜区，2009年被联合国教科文组织列入世界遗产名录。

Mount Wutai

Mount Wutai is located in Wutai county northeast of Shanxi province. It obtained the name from the five flat-top peaks resembling five pillars that support the heaven. The five surrounding mountains make it a place of beautiful scenery and cool climate, attractive to people seeking a summer resort. The Foguang Temple and Nanchan Temple are the two oldest wooden architectures existing now in China. Mount Wutai is regarded as the top of the four famous Buddha Mountains in China and is world-famous for its long history of Buddha culture and ancient architecture groups. Wutai Mountain was listed as a national scenic spot by the State Council in 1982. In June 2009, it was inscribed in the list of the World Heritage as a cultural landscape by UNESCO.

Buddha   [ˈbʊdə]   n. 佛，佛像
heritage [ˈherɪtɪdʒ]   n. 遗产，继承物
inscribe [ɪnˈskraɪb]   v. 登记

四、黄山

黄山是中华民族的又一象征。它以"奇松、怪石、云海、温泉"四绝而闻名天下。它是中国十大风景名胜中唯一一个地处山岳风景区的景区。作为中国山之代表，黄山集中国名山

之大成。著名的地理学家徐霞客曾在游记中写道："五岳归来不看山，黄山归来不看岳。"这也是对黄山的最高评价。同时这里还兼有"天然动物园和天下植物园"之称。现在，美丽的黄山正以它雄奇的风貌迎接着四海宾客。

Mount Huangshan

Mount Huangshan is another symbol of Chinese nation, well-known all around the world for its odd-shaped pines, bizarre rock, cloud sea, and hot springs. It is the only scenic spot of mountains among the Top 10 Scenic Spots in China. As the representative of Chinese mountains, Mount Huangshan has collected all the magnificence of famous mountains in China. As an ancient saying goes, "You won't want to visit any other mountain after seeing Wu Yue, but you won't wish to see even Wu Yue after returning from Mount Huangshan." Also, Mount Huangshan is considered to be a natural zoo and global botanical garden. With its beauty and uniqueness, Mount Huangshan is welcoming visitors from all over the world.

bizarre ［bɪˈzɑːr］ adj. 奇异的
botanical ［bəˈtænɪkl］ adj. 植物的，植物学的

五、秦始皇陵兵马俑

秦始皇陵兵马俑位于秦始皇陵封土以东约 1 500 米处，它是秦始皇陵一个很小的组成部分，目前发现的面积达两万余平方米。兵马俑坑均为地下坑道式土木结构建筑，坑内埋藏有陶质兵马俑七千余件，木质战车一百余辆。兵马俑全部是仿照真人、真马制成。其中，武士面目各异，从服饰、盔甲和排列位置可以很清楚地区分出他们不同的身份。出土的很多武器多为青铜制品，相当一部分至今仍锋利如新。秦始皇陵兵马俑展现了中国古代劳动人民高超的工艺技术和伟大的智慧，被誉为"世界第八大奇迹"。

Terra-cotta Warriors

The site of Terra-cotta Warriors is located about 1 500 meters east of the Qin Shihuang Tomb. As a small part of the Qin Shihuang Tomb, the currently discovered area is larger than 20 000 square meters. All the warrior pits are underground architectures of soil and wood, where buried more than 7 000 pieces of Terra-cotta Warriors and over 100 wooden chariots. Each piece was modeled after real persons and horses. The identities of the warriors, along with diversified facial features, can be clearly distinguished according to their clothes, armors and locations. Most of the weapons found are made of bronze, a remarkable portion of which are still sharp as they were. The Terra-cotta Warriors demonstrate the excellent craftsmanship and great wisdom of the ancient Chinese, and are regarded as one of the eight miracles in the world.

terra-cotta ［ˈterəˈkɒtə］ n. 赤陶土
warrior ［ˈwɔːriər］ n. 勇士，武士
diversified ［daɪˈvɜːsɪfaɪd］ adj. 多样的
distinguish ［dɪˈstɪŋgwɪʃ］ v. 区分
craftsmanship ［ˈkræftsmənʃɪp］ n. 技术，技艺

六、泰山

泰山位于山东省中部的泰安市。风景区面积为两百多平方千米。它是中国古代黄河流域文明的发祥地之一,被誉为"五岳"之首。

泰山山势磅礴雄伟,峰峦突兀峻拔,景色壮丽。中国历代帝王都把泰山当作天的象征,纷纷到此封禅,祭告天地。古代的文人雅士更对泰山仰慕备至,纷纷前来游历,写诗记文,抒发情感。在泰山宏大的山体上共留下了二十多处古建筑群和二千余处碑碣石刻。这都为研究中国古代历史、书法等提供了重要而丰富的实物资料。1987 年,泰山被联合国教科文组织世界遗产委员会列为世界文化、自然双重遗产。泰山不单是一座风景山,更是一座文化山。

Mount Taishan

Mount Taishan, with a scenic area of over 200 square kilometres, is located in Tai'an, a city in the middle of Shandong province. It is one of the birthplaces of the ancient culture along the Yellow River, and is regarded as the first of the Five Sacred Mounts.

Mount Taishan is celebrated for the precipitous peaks and the miraculous scenery. In Chinese history, emperors of the past feudal dynasties would take journey to Mount Taishan, which was considered to be the symbol of heaven, to worship and offer sacrifices to the heaven. Writers and artists had left more than 20 groups of ancient architectures and over 2 000 pieces of calligraphy works when they toured Mount Taishan, which provide plenty of valuable evidences to make research on Chinese ancient history and calligraphy. In 1987, it was listed as the Cultural and Natural Heritage by the World Heritage Center of UNESCO. Mount Taishan is not only a mountain of scenery, but also a mountain of culture.

sacred ['seɪkrɪd] adj. 神圣的

precipitous [prɪ'sɪpɪtəs] adj. 险峻的

sacrifice ['sækrɪfaɪs] n. 祭品,牺牲

七、布达拉宫

雄伟壮观的布达拉宫是拉萨乃至西藏的标志性建筑。在拉萨有这样一句话:到拉萨不参观布达拉宫不算到过拉萨,甚至不算到过西藏。

布达拉宫在拉萨市西北的红山上,是世界上海拔最高,集宫殿、城堡和寺院于一体的宏伟建筑,也是西藏最大、最完整的古代宫堡建筑群,被誉为"世界十大土木建筑之一"。

这里是西藏历代重大宗教和政治仪式的举办地,是古时西藏政教合一的统治中心。布达拉宫始建于公元 7 世纪,是松赞干布为迎娶文成公主而修建的,主体建筑分为白宫和红宫两部分。宫殿高两百余米,外观十三层,内部九层。布达拉宫的正前方是布达拉宫广场,是世界上海拔最高的城市广场。

Potala Palace

The glorious Potala Palace is a symbolic architecture of Lhasa or even Tibet. There is a saying goes like this, "If you missed Potala Palace when visiting Lhasa, you haven't really been to Lhasa, or even Tibet."

The palace is located on the Potala Hill in northwest Lhasa, which is an integration of palaces, castles and temples with the highest altitude in the world. It is also the largest and most complete architecture groups of ancient palaces and castles, thus well-known as one of the ten great architectures in the world.

It has witnessed all the major religious and political ceremonies of generations in Tibet, which made it a regnant center of theocracy in ancient Tibet. The palace was originally built by Songtsen Gampo in the 7th century, in the purpose of marrying Princess Wencheng. The main structures consist of Red Palace and White Palace, with a height of over 200 meters. It has 13 stories when looked from outside and 9 stories from inside. The Potala Square in front of the palace is a city square with the highest altitude in the world.

regnant ['regnənt] adj. 统治的
theocracy [θɪ'ɒkrəsɪ] n. 神权政体
Songtsen Gampo 松赞干布

八、黄果树瀑布

黄果树瀑布位于贵阳以西的白水河上,宽约81米,高约68米,因当地一种常见的植物"黄果树"而得名。河水断崖式地下落,凭高作浪,发出轰然巨响,倾入崖下的犀牛潭中,浪花四溅。远望瀑布,笼罩在轻纱薄雾之中,幻景憧憧。黄果树瀑布以其雄奇壮阔、连环密布的瀑布群而闻名于海内外,并享有"中华第一瀑"的美誉。黄果树瀑布景区已被世界吉尼斯总部评为世界上最大的瀑布群,列入吉尼斯世界纪录。

Huangguoshu Waterfall

The Huangguoshu Waterfall is on the Baishui River, in the west of Guiyang city, about 81 meters in width and 68 meters in height. Its name comes from a common local plant "huangguoshu". The fall runs down in thundering splashes from the 6-8 meters high cliff of the fault of the riverbed into the Rhinoceros Pool, where the water is made to surge with spray splashing. Seen from afar, the waterfall is shrouded in a gauzy mist, looking like a flickering mirage. The gorgeous fall groups bring to it the great fame of "the top fall in China". The scenic area has been graded and listed as the world's largest fall group by the Guinness World headquarter.

fault [fɔːlt] n. 断层
surge [sɜːdʒ] v. 汹涌,涌起
shroud [ʃraʊd] v. 覆盖,遮蔽
mirage [məˈrɑːʒ] n. 幻景

九、长江三峡

举世闻名的长江三峡是中国十大风景名胜之一,是瞿塘峡、巫峡和西陵峡三段峡谷的总称。三峡地跨湖北、重庆两省市。两岸崇山峻岭,气势恢宏,风景秀丽。三峡东起湖北宜昌市,西至重庆奉节白帝城,被中外游客誉为"山水画廊"。

The Yangtze Gorges

The Yangtze Gorges are one of the top 10 scenic spots in China, referred to as Qutang Gorge, Wu Gorge and Xiling Gorge and boast splendid vigor and picturesque views. Starting from Yichang City in Hubei province to Baidi Town in Fengjie in Chongqing, they are dubbed as the "Gallery of Water and Mountain" by tourists home and abroad.

picturesque ［ˌpɪktʃəˈresk］ adj. 如画的，生动的

十、峨眉山

峨眉山位于四川省乐山市境内，景区面积约 154 平方千米，最高峰万佛顶海拔 3 000 余米。这里层峦叠嶂，山势雄伟，景色秀丽，气象万千。这里是人类文化的宝库，文化遗产极其丰富，是中国佛教圣地，被誉为"佛国天堂"，为中国四大佛教名山之一。作为普贤菩萨的道场，主要供奉普贤大士，有寺庙约 26 座。峨眉山以其秀丽的自然风光、迷人的景色而享有"峨眉天下秀"的美称。

Mount Emei

Mount Emei is located in Leshan city of Sichuan province, with a scenic area of 154 square kilometers. The altitude of its main peak, Wanfoding, is over 3 000 meters. It is well-known for gorgeous mountain ranges, beautiful scenery, and diversified climates. With a splendid cultural legacy, it is regarded as a holy Buddha place in China. Mount Emei is one of the four famous Chinese mountains of Buddha with 26 temples, serving as the rites of Samantabhadra. Mount Emei has won its fame as "the greatest beauty under heaven" thanks to its charming natural scenery.

rite ［raɪt］ n. 仪式，道场
Samantabhadra n. 普贤菩萨

十一、衡山

衡山又名南岳，为我国五岳名山之一，位于湖南中部衡阳市。山脉绵延约 150 千米，有七十二高峰。南端起于回雁峰，北端止于岳麓山。其最高峰为祝融峰，海拔约 1 300.2 米。衡山气候温和，处处是茂林修竹，终年翠绿，奇花异草，四季飘香，自然景色十分秀丽。

Mount Hengshan

Mount Hengshan, named the Southern Mountain of the Five Sacred Mountains, is located in Hengyang, in the middle of Hunan province. It has 72 peaks and extends 150 kilometers. The south of it starts from the Huiyan Peak and the north ends in Yuelu Mountain. The Zhurong Peak is the highest, with an altitude of 1 300.2 meters. The mild climates here bring about dense forest that is ever green all the year.

十二、恒山

恒山风景名胜区位于山西省大同市境内，与东岳泰山、西岳华山、南岳衡山、中岳嵩山并称为"五岳"。恒山自然景观独特，有"人天北柱"的美称，景区内的悬空寺是国内为数不

多的佛、道、儒"三教合一"的独特寺庙,整座寺院好似悬在峭壁上,下临深谷,楼阁悬空,蔚为壮观。清代时恒山已经寺庙成群,人们称之为"三寺四祠九亭阁,七宫八洞十二庙",具有重要的历史研究价值。1982年恒山风景名胜区被国务院列为第一批国家级风景名胜区。

Mount Hengshan

Located in Datong city of Shanxi province, Hengshan Mountain is regarded as one of the five greatest mountains in China, with the other four as Mount Taishan in the east, Mount Huashan in the west, Mount Hengshan in the south, Mount Songshan in central China. In the spot, the Xuankong (suspended) Temple is the only existing temple in China combining Buddhism, Taoism and Confucianism together. Constructed on a section of a cliff, the temple is truly a masterpiece of ancient structure. The temples reached a notable scale back in Qing Dynasty, and now is valuable in research of history and culture. Mount Hengshan was listed as the national scenic spot by the State Council in 1982.

reputation　　[ˌrepjuˈteɪʃən]　　n. 好名声,声誉
heritage　　[ˈherɪtɪdʒ]　　n. 遗产,继承物
Taoism　　[ˈtaʊɪzəm]　　n. 道教
Confucianism　　[kənˈfjuːʃənɪzm]　　n. 孔子思想,儒家思想

十三、庐山

庐山位于江西省九江市,北濒长江,南临鄱阳湖,山体呈椭圆形,约有90座山峰,犹如九叠屏风。主峰汉阳峰,海拔1 474米。宋代诗人苏轼曾发出"不识庐山真面目,只缘身在此山中"的感慨。深厚的文化底蕴、奇特的地质地貌、变幻的自然气候现象、丰富的生态资源,构成了庐山旅游的特色。庐山风景以雄、奇、险、秀闻名于世,具有极高的科学研究价值和旅游观赏价值。同时,这里也是著名的避暑胜地。

Mount Lushan

Mount Lushan is located in Jiujiang city of Jiangxi province, with the Yangtze River to the north and Poyang Lake to the south. The mountain is of an oval shape with the main peak Han Yang of 1 474 meters. Sushi, the famous poet in the Song Dynasty, when visiting Mount Lushan, once wrote,"How could one tell what Mount Lushan really looks like when one is in the midst of the mountain all along?"As a famous tourism spot, Mount Lushan is especially famous for its rich cultural ethos, unique geological structure, varied natural climate, and rich ecological resources, all of which make colorful paintings of Mount Lushan and make it a well-known summer resort.

ethos　　[ˈiːθɒs]　　n. 民族精神,道德风貌,风气
ecological　　[ˌiːkəˈlɒdʒɪkl]　　adj. 生态的,生态学的

十四、武夷山

武夷山位于福建省武夷山市南郊,是集国家级重点风景名胜区、国家级旅游度假区、国家级自然保护区于一体的著名旅游胜地。占地约999平方千米,是典型的丹霞地貌。武夷

山以其丰富的自然生态资源、独特的自然风光、灿烂悠久的历史文化，以及和谐的环境而著称，素有"碧水丹山"的美誉，是中国旅游胜地之一。武夷山于1996年12月被联合国教科文组织列为世界自然文化遗产。

Mount Wuyi

Mount Wuyi is situated in the Wuyishan city, the northern part of Fujian province. The main site is about 999 square kilometers, and is typical Danxia landform. It is the only place in China that has been elected as the national key tourist resort, national tourist holiday resort, and national nature reserve. Mount Wuyi is well-known for its abundant natural resources, unique natural scenery, brilliant historical culture, and harmonious environment. It is considered to be one of the best resorts for tourism in China. In December 1996, Mount Wuyi was honored as World's Cultural and Natural Heritage by UNESCO.

brilliant ['brɪliənt] adj. 卓越的，灿烂的，美妙的
harmonious [hɑː'məʊniəs] adj. 和谐的，和睦的

十五、西湖

西湖位于杭州市西部，三面环山，是中国首批国家重点风景名胜区和中国十大风景名胜之一。西湖不仅风景如画，而且在这里还可以找到很多学者和英雄的遗迹，岳王庙、白堤、苏堤、雷峰塔等都是著名的旅游景点。这些古建筑也是中国最珍贵的历史遗产，具有较高的艺术价值和历史价值。

West Lake

West Lake is located in the western area of Hangzhou city. Surrounded by mountains on three sides, it is one of the ten famous scenic spots of China and listed in the first batch of the national key scenic resorts. West Lake is not only famous for its picturesque landscape, it is also associated with many scholars and national heroes. Renowned tourist attractions include Yue Fei Temple, Bai Causeway, Su Causeway, and Leifeng Tower, ect. In addition, many ancient buildings in surrounding areas are among the most cherished national treasures with significant artistic value.

十六、黄河壶口瀑布

壶口瀑布位于山西省九曲黄河中游，是全国第二大瀑布。黄河流经此处河槽由宽300余米突然变窄为30余米，聚集的河水流入深潭，落差20米，像是茶壶在注水，所以叫作壶口瀑布。浪涛滚滚的河水排山倒海般涌来，到此处合拢，惊涛拍岸，似雷霆轰鸣。在水量大的夏季，壶口瀑布气势恢宏。而到了冬季，整个水面全部冰冻，结出罕见的巨大冰瀑。

The Hukou Waterfalls of the Yellow River

The Hukou Waterfalls of the Yellow River is located in the middle of the nine-curve Yellow River in Shanxi province. It is the second largest waterfall in China. The river narrows and cascades dramatically into a stone pond more than 30 meters below, creating the famous Hukou Waterfalls. The gentle water becomes turbulent and gains speed as it rushed forward till it finally cascades over the waterfall, forming an illusion of water being poured from a kettle, hence its name is "Hukou or Kettle spout". Like thousands of tumbling dragons or enraged animals that have just been set free, the yellow water plunged down, the pounding against the stones echoes like thunder. The water surface freezes all over in winter, creating a rare giant ice waterfall.

cascade ［kæˈskeɪd］ v. 瀑布似的落下
turbulent ［ˈtɜːbjələnt］ adj. 狂暴的,骚动的,动荡的,汹涌的
kettle ［ˈketl］ n. 水壶,坑穴
tumbling ［ˈtʌmblɪŋ］ adj. 翻腾的
plunge ［plʌndʒ］ v. 使投入,跳入,栽进
pounding ［ˈpaʊndɪŋ］ n. 重击声,猛击

 任务五 城市介绍

一、哈尔滨

哈尔滨是黑龙江省省会,也是中国东北政治、经济、交通、文化中心。哈尔滨是中国历史文化名城、热点旅游城市和国际冰雪文化名城。特殊的历史背景和地理位置造就了哈尔滨这座具有异国情调的美丽城市,它不仅荟萃了北方少数民族的文化,而且融合了中外文化,被誉为欧亚大陆桥的明珠,是欧亚大陆桥和空中走廊的重要枢纽,素有"冰城""天鹅颈下的珍珠"及"东方莫斯科"的美称。

Harbin

Harbin is the capital of Heilongjiang Province. It is also the political, economic, transportation and cultural center of northeast China. Harbin is a historical and cultural city in China, and a famous ice and snow tourist city. Special geographical location and historical background help to make Harbin a beautiful city of exoticism. The culture of north minorities and those of other countries are assembled harmoniously here, to make it a famous Chinese tourist city and a city of history and culture. It is a major city of the Eurasia Land Bridge and aviation hub, also known as "Ice City", "Pearl on the neck of swan", and "Oriental Moscow".

exoticism ［ɪgˈzɒtɪsɪzəm］ n. 异国情调
Eurasia Land Bridge 欧亚大陆桥

二、长春

长春是吉林省省会,地处中国东北松辽平原中部,面积约 20 571 平方千米,是中国东

北第二大城市和吉林省政治、经济和文化中心。如果把中国版图看作一只大公鸡，长春的位置就是这只大公鸡的眼睛。同时，长春也是新中国汽车工业、生物技术、电影科技的发祥地。长春地处湿润区与半干燥区的过渡地带，这里长年受季风气候影响，四季分明，气候宜人，长久以来被称作"北国春城"。

Changchun

Changchun is located in the central part of Songliao Plain in Northeast China, covering a total area of 20 571 square kilometers. As the capital of Jilin Province, it is the second largest city in Northeast China and the political, economic and cultural center of the province. If the territory of China is in a shape of rooster, Changchun is one eye of this huge rooster. You can imagine its important position. It is the birthplace of the auto industry, bio-technology, and movie technology of China. Changchun is of monsoon climate, locating in the transitional belt from wet area to sub-dry area. The four seasons vary a lot and the climate is rather pleasant, therefore it is honored as the spring city of north land.

territory　　[ˈterətrɪ]　　n. 领土，领域，版图
monsoon　　[ˌmɒnˈsuːn]　　n. 季风
transitional　　[trænˈzɪʃənl]　　adj. 过渡的

三、沈阳

沈阳是辽宁省省会，是全省政治、经济和文化中心。位于中国东北地区南部，面积约13 000平方千米。沈阳是国家园林城市和历史文化名城，有两千多年的建城史，也是中国著名的工业城市，是中国最重要的以装备制造业为主的重工业基地，有"东方鲁尔"的美誉。

Shenyang

Shenyang is the capital city and the political, economic and cultural center of Liaoning Province, as well as a famous city of heavy industry. Covering an area of about 13 000 square kilometers, it has long history of more than 2 000 years. It's not only a famous garden city and historical city in China, but also a well-known industrial city. Shenyang is a major heavy plant base in China, focusing on equipment manufacturing. It enjoys the fame of "Oriental Ruhr".

四、大连

大连是我国著名的沿海游览和疗养胜地，位于辽东半岛南端，与山东半岛隔海相望，是我国主要工业城市之一。大连港也是我国对外贸易港和重要渔业基地。大连海滨风光明媚，名胜有老虎滩公园及星海公园等。大连环境绝佳，气候冬无严寒，夏无酷暑，有"北方明珠"之称，是中国东北对外开放的窗口和最大的港口城市，先后获得"国际花园城市""中国最佳旅游城市"等荣誉。

Dalian

Dalian is well-known as a coastal tourism and health resort. It is located in the south end of Liaodong Peninsula. Dalian is one of the major industrial cities in China. Dalian Harbor is also an important foreign trade harbor and a fishery base. Dalian has beautiful coastal scenic resorts, such as Tiger Beach, Xinghai Beach, and so on. The excellent location and mild climate have won its name as "Pearl of Northern China". It is the window of opening to the outside world and the largest port city of northeastern China. Dalian has been awarded with the titles of International Garden City, Best Tourism City of China, etc.

peninsula ［pəˈnɪnsjələ］ n. 半岛

五、呼和浩特

呼和浩特是内蒙古自治区省会,是内蒙古的经济、文化、科教和金融中心。呼和浩特位于内蒙古中部,面积约6 200平方千米,是中国向蒙古、俄罗斯开放的重要中心城市,也是东部地区连接西北、华北的枢纽城市。呼和浩特有着悠久的历史和光辉灿烂的文化,是华夏文明的发祥地之一。这里的城市建筑风格独特,古今辉映,别有韵味,共有三十多个不同民族聚居于此。呼和浩特草原畜牧业发达,被誉为"中国乳都"。

Hohhot

Hohhot is the capital city and the center of economy, culture, education and finance of Inner Mongolia Autonomous Region. Located in the middle of Inner Mongolia, Hohhot is a major central city of China opening to Mongolia and Russia, and a key city connecting the northwestern and northern China. Hohhot has a long history and brilliant culture. The architectures are unique in style. More than 30 ethnics live here. The developed grassland animal husbandry has won it a name as the "Dairy Center of China".

Hohhot ［ˈhəuˈhɔt］ n. 呼和浩特(内蒙古自治区省会)
Mongolian ［mɒŋˈɡəulɪən］ adj. 蒙古人的,蒙古语的
animal husbandry 畜牧业

六、北京

北京是中华人民共和国的首都,是我国的政治、文化、教育中心,也是我国最重要的国际贸易与交流中心。北京与西安、洛阳、开封、南京及杭州并称"六大古都"。自秦朝以来,北京一直作为北方乃至全国的政治中心。游客至此,无不沉醉于北京灿烂的历史文化与现代化的城市发展。北京的主要景点有故宫、颐和园、天坛、长城等。

Beijing

Beijing, capital of China, is China's political, cultural and educational center as well as China's most important center for international trade and communications. Together with Xi'an, Luoyang, Kaifeng, Nanjing and Hangzhou, Beijing is one of the six ancient cities in China. It has been the political center throughout its long history since the Qin Dynasty and consequently there is an unparalleled wealth of discovery to delight and intrigue travelers as they explore Beijing's ancient past and enjoy its exciting modern

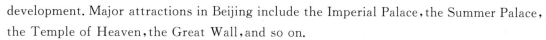

development. Major attractions in Beijing include the Imperial Palace, the Summer Palace, the Temple of Heaven, the Great Wall, and so on.

unparalleled ［ʌnˈpærəleld］ adj. 无比的，无双的
intrigue ［ɪnˈtriːg］ v. 激起……的兴趣

七、天津

天津是我国四个直辖市之一，地处华北平原东北部，是我国首都北京的门户。天津位于海河下游，地跨海河两岸，是北京通往东北、华东地区的交通咽喉和远洋航运的重要港口，是中国北方最大的沿海开放城市。市内景点有天津广播电视塔、水上公园、天后宫等。还有许多具有英、法、意等国风格的历史建筑。南市食品街汇集了祖国各地的代表美食，使天津成为一座别具特色的美食城市。

Tianjin

Tianjin, located in the northeast of Huabei Plain, is regarded as the gate to the capital of China. It is one of the four municipalities in China. Tianjin is well-known as a major industrial city and harbor in the North as well as an important outlet to the sea. Major attractions include Tianjin TV Tower, Water Park, Tianhou Palace, and so on. There are also many old buildings of English, French, and Italian styles. The Nanshi Food Bazaar gathers delicacies from all around China and makes Tianjin a unique city of cuisine.

municipality ［mjuːˌnɪsɪˈpælətɪ］ n. 自治市
bazaar ［bəˈzɑː］ n. 市集，商场，义卖的地方
delicacy ［ˈdelɪkəsɪ］ n. 精致，优雅，佳肴
cuisine ［kwɪˈziːn］ n. 烹饪，佳肴

八、太原

太原是山西省省会，濒临汾河，三面环山，是全省政治、经济、文化、交通中心。太原有两千多年的建城史，是国家历史文化名城、国家园林城市。太原是中国能源、重工业基地之一，冶金、机械、化工等在全国都有举足轻重的地位，其煤矿产量占全国一半以上。太原旅游资源丰富，特别是晋祠，是太原最有名的景点。另外，双塔寺以其独特的建筑特点，成为太原的象征。

Taiyuan

Taiyuan, the capital of Shanxi Province, is near Fen River and surrounded on three sides by mountains. It is the center of politics, economy, culture and transport of the province. Taiyuan has a history of more than two thousand years, it is a famous historical and cultural city, and a national garden city. Now Taiyuan is one of China's heavy industrial cities and accounts for more than half of the national coal mining output. Taiyuan also has a lot of tourist attractions and notably among these is the Jinci Temple. This is the city's most attractive temple. Double-tower Temple is another resort for its unique architecture features.

九、济南

济南是山东省省会，是山东省政治、经济、文化中心，有两千多年的悠久历史，是中华文明的发祥地之一。济南位于黄河之南、大明湖畔，自然风光秀丽，因其境内泉水众多而有"泉城"的美称。济南有四大名泉群，包括趵突泉、黑虎泉、珍珠泉、五龙潭等，合称"七十二名泉"。另外还有千佛山、四门塔、红叶谷等著名景点。济南被评为"首批中国优秀旅游城市"。

Jinan

Jinan is the capital of Shandong Province as well as its political, economic, and cultural center. Jinan has a long history of over 2 000 years. It is one of the birthplaces of Chinese civilization. Jinan is also known for its beautiful natural scenery, and it has got a laudatory name "City of Springs" because of the numerous springs scattered over the city. There are four spring groups including Baotu Spring, Black Tiger Spring, Pearl Spring, and Wulongtan Spring as well as other minor groups in suburbs. These springs are known as "the famous 72 springs". Other attractions are Qianfo Mountain, Simen Pagoda, Hongye Valley, etc. With its well-known resorts, Jinan was one of the first national excellent tourist cities.

laudatory ['lɔ:dətərɪ] adj. 赞美的，赞赏的

十、青岛

青岛地处山东半岛东南部，东、南濒临黄海。青岛依山傍海，风光秀丽，气候宜人。红瓦、绿树、碧海、蓝天交相映出青岛美丽的海滨风情。赤礁、细浪、彩帆、金色沙滩构成青岛美丽的海岸风景线。青岛是全国首批沿海开放城市、国家历史文化名城、全国文明城市。青岛因海鲜而闻名。悠久的历史也赋予了青岛丰富的文化内涵，栈桥、五四广场、八大关和道教圣地崂山等是青岛的著名景点。典型欧式风格的各国建筑，有的造型迥异，有的古朴凝重，有的清幽典雅，形成了中西合璧的特色。

Qingdao

Qingdao is located in the southeast of Shandong Peninsula with the Yellow Sea to the east and south. It has beautiful scenery and pleasant climate. It looks like a harmonious picture painted with mountains, sea and city, where we can see the winding and beautiful buildings whose red roofs are held in the embrace of verdant trees. Qingdao is one of the first cities in China opening up to the outside world, and is a famous city of history and culture. Qingdao is famous in China for its delicious fresh seafood. The Landing Stage, May 4 Square, Badaguan and Taoist shrine Mount Laoshan are famous scenic spots in Qingdao. There are many European-style buildings, which are combinations of Chinese and Western culture.

embrace [ɪm'breɪs] n. 拥抱

verdant ['vɜːdnt] adj. 翠绿的

十一、郑州

郑州是河南省省会,地处华北平原南部,河南省中部偏北,北临黄河,西依嵩山,东南为广阔的黄淮平原,是全省政治、经济、科技中心。郑州是全国重要的铁路、航空、高速公路、电力、邮政枢纽城市。郑州历史悠久,文化灿烂,是中华文明的发源地。早在3 500年前的商代,郑州就是一个重要的城市。悠久的历史和灿烂的文明造就了这座城市丰富的人文景观,全市各类文物古迹达一万余处,著名的景点有黄帝故里、黄河游览区、商城遗址、嵩山少林寺等。

Zhengzhou, the capital of Henan Province, is located in the south of the Northern China Plain, with Yellow River to its north, Mount Songshan to its west and Huang Huai Plain to its southeast. It is the center of politics, economy, science and technology of the province. Zhengzhou is a major city of railway, aviation, expressway, electric power, and post. Zhengzhou has a long history and is the one of the birthplaces of Chinese Civilization. It was an important city 3 500 years ago in Shang Dynasty. These have left the city with abundant scenic spots of humanity. There are more than 10 000 relics, including the HuangDi's hometown, the Yellow River Resort, the relic of Shang capital, and Shaolin Temple.

十二、洛阳

洛阳位于河南省西部,因其地处古洛水之阳而得其名。其历史可追溯至三千多年前。洛阳是"十三朝古都",有着深厚的文化底蕴,有一千五百多年的建都史,先后有一百多位帝王在此定鼎九州。洛阳是国务院公布的第一批古都城市与历史文化名城之一。这里名胜古迹众多,有白马寺、龙门石窟、白云山、邙山等风景名胜。牡丹是洛阳这座城市的名片,每年这里还举办中国洛阳牡丹文化节,牡丹因洛阳而闻名于天下,洛阳又被誉为"千年帝都""牡丹花城",每年都吸引着大批国内外游客。

Luoyang

Located in the west of Henan Province, Luoyang got its name due to its location in the south direction of the ancient Luoshui River. It is a historical city with more than three thousand years. Luoyang has been known as "an ancient capital of thirteen dynasties". More than 100 emperors has chosen it to be the capital. It is among the first cities to be declared by the State Council as the ancient capitals and famous historical and cultural cities. The famous scenic resorts include the White Horse Temple, Longmen Rock Caves, Baiyun Mountain and Mount Mangshan. Peony is the name card of the city. The yearly festival of Luoyang Peony is well-known all around and attracts lots of tourists from home and abroad.

十三、南京

南京是江苏省省会,全省政治、经济、文化中心,面积约6 587平方千米。南京是中国著名的七大古都及历史文化名城之一。南京依山傍水,古迹众多,既有自然山水之胜,又有历史文物之雅。名胜古迹有中山陵、明孝陵和灵古寺,还有玄武湖、燕子矶、莫愁湖等风景名胜。

Nanjing

Nanjing is the capital of Jiangsu Province as well as its political, economic and cultural center. It covers 6 587 square kilometers. Nanjing is known as one of the seven ancient capitals and historical and cultural cities in China. Near Zijin Mountain and by the Yangtze River, Nanjing is abundant in natural, historical and cultural scenic spots, including Dr. Sun Yat Sen's Mausoleum, Ming Tomb and Linggu Temple. Other places of interest include Xuanwu Lake, Yanziji, and Mochou Lake.

十四、合肥

合肥是安徽省省会,是全省政治、经济、文化中心,位于安徽省中部,长江、淮河之间,面积约11 445平方千米。合肥有"绿色之城"的美称,淝水河穿城而过,形成了"城在园中,园在城中"的独特花园城市风貌。合肥自然景色锦绣多姿,文化古迹众多,包公祠、天鹅湖、四顶山、逍遥津等都是这座城市的风景名胜。

Hefei is the capital and the center of politics, economy and culture of Anhui Province. It is located right in the center of the province and between the Yangtze River and Huai River, with an area of about 11 445 square kilometers. Hefei is known as the "Green City". Feishui River winds through the city, and gives it a unique appearance of garden city. The cultural relics include Baogong Temple, Swan Lake, Siding Mountain and Xiaoyaojin.

十五、武汉

武汉是湖北省省会,是全省政治、经济、文化中心,面积约8 569平方千米。武汉位于中国中部,地处江汉平原东部,地理位置十分优越,是中国内陆最大的水陆空综合交通枢纽,是连接东西南北的地理中心,历来有"九省通衢"之称。武汉是一座典型的山水园林城市,上百座大小山峦遍布全城,近两百个湖泊坐落其间,水域面积占全市面积的四分之一。武汉旅游景点有天下第一楼黄鹤楼、中国最大城中湖东湖、佛教圣地归元寺、万里长江第一桥武汉长江大桥等。

Wuhan

Wuhan is the capital and the center of politics, economy and culture of Hubei Province, with an area of about 8 569 square kilometers. Wuhan has an excellent location and thus is the largest comprehensive transportation center in inland China, which connects the important parts of China in all directions. Wuhan therefore is called "the thoroughfare to nine provinces". Wuhan is a typical garden city with hundreds of mountains and waters. The water area accounts for one fourth of that of the whole city. The scenic resorts include Yellow Crane Tower, East Lake, Guiyuan Temple, and the Wuhan Yangtze River Bridge.

十六、长沙

长沙是湖南省省会,是全省政治、经济、文化中心,面积约 11 819 平方千米。长沙位于中国中南部,气候温暖,依山带水,有"山水名郡"之称。长沙旅游资源丰富,悠久的历史和秀丽的风景使长沙境内名胜遍布。岳麓山、马王堆、开福寺、天心阁、橘子洲等都是这座城市的著名景点。长沙小吃也以辣闻名于世。

Changsha

Changsha is located in the east of Hunan Province in mid-south China. It is known for its warm climate and is the economic and political center of the province. As a large city, Changsha covers an area of 11 819 square kilometers and is known as a "famous city of mountain and water". Major attractions in Changsha include Yuelu Mountain, Mawangdui Han Tombs, Kaifu Temple, Tianxin Pavilion, Orange Island, and so on. Changsha is also well-known for its spicy snacks.

十七、南昌

南昌是江西省省会,是全省政治、经济、文化中心,是赣江流域的第一大都市。南昌地处江西省中部,赣江下游,濒临鄱阳湖,既是国家历史文化名城,又是革命英雄城。南昌自然风光秀丽,人文景观众多,位于市中心八一广场上的八一南昌起义纪念塔,是南昌革命历史的丰碑和象征。南昌周边有著名的世界文化遗产庐山风景名胜区、鄱阳湖候鸟保护区、龙虎山、井冈山。

Nanchang

Nanchang is the capital and the center of politics, economy and culture of Jiangxi Province. It is located in the middle of the province. It's not only a famous national city of history and culture, but also a city of revolutionary heroes. The Monument of Nanchang Uprising in Bayi Square is the symbol of the revolutionary history of Nanchang. Famous scenic resorts include Mount Lushan Resort, Poyang Lake Migrating Birds Reserve, Longhu Mountain, and Jinggangshan National Resort.

十八、杭州

杭州是浙江省省会,是全省的政治、经济、文化和金融中心,位于中国东南沿海、浙江省北部、钱塘江下游、京杭大运河南端。杭州也是中国最著名的风景旅游城市之一,被誉为"东南第一州",素有"上有天堂,下有苏杭"的美誉。市内人文古迹众多,西湖、钱塘江、雷峰塔、岳王庙等都是著名的风景名胜。

Hangzhou

Hangzhou is the capital and the center of politics, economy and culture of Zhejiang Province. It is located in the southeastern coast of China, the north of the province, in the downstream section of the Qiantang River, and the southern end of the Beijing-Hangzhou Grand Canal. It is one of the national key tourism cities and is reputed as "the first state in southeast China". Hangzhou is one of the most famous tourism cities in China, and it has long been praised as "Paradise in Heaven, Suzhou and Hangzhou on Earth". There are abundant sites of culture and history, including the West Lake, Qiantang River, Leifeng Tower, and Yue Fei Temple.

十九、上海

上海市地处我国东部沿海,长江入海口,是我国四个直辖市之一,同时也是我国最大的城市,是我国国家中心城市,中国经济、金融、贸易、航运中心。上海是全国著名的商业和旅游城市,是一座极具现代化而又不失中国传统特色的国际大都市。百余年来,上海一直是中国商业的中心、财富的汇聚地。上海旅游资源丰富,外滩、南京路、豫园、朱家角古镇等都是这座现代化大都市的风景名胜,黄浦江畔高耸入云的东方明珠广播电视塔更成为上海的标志性建筑。

Shanghai

Shanghai is located in the east coast of China and the estuary of the Yangtze River. It is one of the four municipalities in China as well as China's largest city. Shanghai is a national central city as well as the center of economy, finance, trade and shipping in China. As a famous national city of commerce and tourism, Shanghai integrates both modern and traditional features and becomes an international metropolis. It has been the commercial center and land of fortune for more than 100 years. The scenic resorts include The Bund, Nanjing Road, Yu Garden, and Zhujiajiao Ancient Town. The Oriental Pearl TV Tower near Huangpu River has become a landmark building in Shanghai.

二十、福州

福州是福建省省会,是海峡西岸经济区政治、经济、文化、科研中心以及现代金融服务业中心,位于福建省东部、闽江下游,东濒东海。福州背山依江面海,气候宜人,地理环境优越,有"温泉城"的雅称,还有"江南胜地"的美誉。福州是中国优秀旅游城市,国家园林城市,山清水秀,风景秀丽,名山、名寺、名园繁多,平潭海坛、鼓山、青云山、十八重溪等都是福州的风景名胜。

Fuzhou

Fuzhou is the capital city of Fujian Province and the center of politics, economy, culture, research and modern finance service of the west coast of Taiwan Strait. It is located in the downstream section of Minjiang River, bordering the East Sea in the east. With mountains at back and sea in the front, this city enjoys amicable climate and excellent environment. It is reputed as the "City of Hot Spring" and "Resort in south of the Yangtze River district". Fuzhou is a national excellent tourist city with lots of famous mountains, temples and gardens, including Pingtanhaitan, Gushan Mountain, Qingyun

Mountain and Shibachong Stream.

二十一、广州

广州是广东省省会,别称"羊城""花城"。广州是中国历史文化名城,两千多年来一直都是华南地区的政治、军事、经济、文化和科教中心。广州也是海上丝绸之路的起点,被称为中国的"南大门"。广州地处广东省中部、珠江三角洲北部,濒临中国南海,跨珠江两岸,是我国华南地区最大的城市和经济贸易中心。广州素以名胜古迹众多而闻名,主要有镇海楼、南越王墓、陈家祠、六榕寺、光孝寺等景点。四季如春的气候,如画的美丽风光,悠久的名胜古迹,别具风味的名菜佳肴,都令游人流连忘返。

Guangzhou

Guangzhou, also known as "City of Goats" and "City of Flowers", is a famous ancient city with a history of over 2 000 years as the politic, military, economic, cultural and educational center of southern China. It is the beginning of the Maritime Silk Road and is called the "South Gate" of China. Guangzhou is located in the middle of the Guangdong Province and north of the Pearl River Delta, bordering the South China Sea, with the Pearl River flowing through. It is the largest city and the economic and trade center in south China. There are renowned scenic spots and historic resorts, such as Zhenhai Tower, Tomb of Nanyuewang, Chen's Lineage Hall, Liurong Temple, and Guangxiao Temple, etc. Guangzhou is famous for its year-round spring and beautiful scenery, historic monuments, and the unique flavor of specialty.

二十二、南宁

南宁是广西壮族自治区的首府,是自治区政治、经济、文化中心。南宁位于广西西南地区,拥有优越的地理位置,西接中南半岛,东临粤港澳琼,不仅是环北部湾沿岸重要的经济中心,也是新崛起的大西南出海通道枢纽城市。南宁是一座历史悠久的边陲古城,具有深厚的文化积淀。南宁市的旅游资源十分丰富,这里山、河、湖、溪与绿树鲜花交相辉映,亚热带的自然风光与现代园林城市的风貌融为一体,形成了独特的南国城市风景。南宁有着全国最高的城市绿化覆盖率,享有"中国绿城"的美誉。

Nanning

Nanning, the capital city of Guangxi Zhuang Autonomous Region and is the center of politics, economy and culture of Guangxi, enjoys a favorable geographical location, connecting the Indo-China Peninsula to the west and Guangdong Province, Hong Kong, Macao and Hainan Province to the east, making it not only an important economic center at the Beibu Gulf, but also a rapid growing gateway city to Southeast Asia and southwestern parts of China. Nanning is a frontier city with a long history and cultural legacy. It is abundant in tourist resources, mountains, rivers, lakes. The city is featured in the natural scenery of subtropics and it enjoys the reputation of the "Green City of China" because of its best green coverage in the country.

二十三、桂林

桂林是世界著名的风景游览城市和历史文化名城。桂林市地处南岭山系的西南部,平均海拔150米,属于典型的"喀斯特"岩溶地貌。这里千峰环立、一水抱城、洞奇石美,有"桂林山水甲天下"的美誉。其中最具有代表性的景点有象鼻山、尧山、独秀峰、七星岩、榕湖等。这里"江作青罗带,山如碧玉簪"的美景,令人流连忘返。

Guilin

Guilin, a world-famous scenic city, is located in the southwest of Nanling Mountains, with an average altitude of 150 meters. The typical karst landscape gives Guilin thousands of unique hills, rivers and caves. As a saying goes, "Guilin's scenery is the finest under heaven". The representative scenic spots include Elephant Trunk Hill, Yao Hill, Solitary Beauty Peak, Seven-Star Cave, and the Ronghu Lake. The beauty of the rivers and hills have attracted lots of tourists.

二十四、海口

海口为海南省省会,是海南省政治、文化、经济、交通中心。因地处海南岛北端,为南渡江入海口,故名海口。海口北临琼州海峡,与雷州半岛遥相对峙。年平均气温23.8 ℃,水碧天蓝、长夏无冬,全城遍植椰树。名胜有五公祠、琼台书院、海瑞墓以及众多风光秀丽的海滨浴场。

Haikou

Haikou, the capital of Hainan Province, is also the political, cultural, economic, and transportation center. It is located in the northern end of Hainan Island, and is the sea outfall of Nandu River. That's how it got its name as Haikou. With Qiongzhou Strait to the north, it faces Leizhou Peninsula across the sea. The annual average temperature there is 23.8 ℃. With clear water and blue sky, summer stays there all year long. Coconut trees are planted all over the city. The attractions are Wugong Memorial Tower, Qiongtai Academy, Hairui Tomb and various seaside resorts.

二十五、乌鲁木齐

乌鲁木齐是新疆维吾尔自治区的省会,是新疆的政治、经济、文化中心,中国西部对外开放的重要门户。它位于天山北麓,环山绕水,沃野广袤。天山山脉分布着高山冰雪景观、山地森林景观、草原景观,为游客观光、探险提供了丰富的资源,各民族的文化艺术和风情习俗构成了具有民族特色的人文景观。这里是举世闻名的"丝绸之路"的必经之路,现在,丝绸之路冰雪风情游、丝绸之路服装服饰节等带有"丝绸之路"文化特色的节庆活动,已成为乌鲁木齐特有的城市名片。

Urumqi

Urumqi is the capital of the Xinjiang Uygur Autonomous Region as well as its political, economic, and cultural center. It is an important gateway of opening-up of western China. It is located in the Tianshan Mountains. Surrounded with mountains and water, there are resorts of ice and snow on high mountains, forests, and grasslands, providing tourists with ample resources of sightseeing and exploration. It was a place that the world-famous "Silk Road" must pass. The cultural features of the Silk Road and other festivals have brought Urumqi unique characteristics.

Urumqi   n. 乌鲁木齐

二十六、西宁

西宁是青海省省会,是全省政治、经济、文化中心。西宁位于青海省东部,具有悠久的历史文化,是"唐蕃古道"的必经之地,素有"海藏咽喉"之称,是世界海拔最高的城市之一。丰富的自然资源和多彩的传统文化,使西宁成为青藏高原上一颗璀璨的明珠,主要旅游景点有青海湖、塔尔寺、东关清真寺等。

Xining

Xining is the capital and the political, economic, cultural center of Qinghai Province. It is located in the east of Qinghai Province and serves as the eastern gate of the Qinghai-Tibet Plateau. It has a source of long history and culture, with the "Ancient Tang Bo Passage" passing here. It is also one of the cities with the highest altitude in the world. With a source of abundant natural resources and colorful traditions, Xining has become a shining pearl on the Qinghai-Tibet Plateau. The major tourist attractions include the Qinghai Lake, Ta'er Temple and Dongguan Mosque.

二十七、兰州

兰州是甘肃省省会,是全省政治、经济、文化中心。兰州是西北地区重要的工业基地和综合交通枢纽,是西部地区重要的中心城市之一。兰州是黄河流域唯一一个黄河穿城而过的省会城市,市区依山傍水,山静水动,形成了独特而美丽的城市景观。黄河水的滋养,使得兰州成为驰名中外的瓜果名城,夏秋季节更是具有避暑和品瓜果的旅游特色。兰州是历史文化名城,名胜古迹主要有吐鲁沟、石佛、五泉山、白塔山等。

Lanzhou

Lanzhou, the capital and the political, economic, cultural center of Gansu Province, is a central city in Northwest China. It is the only provincial capital where the Yellow River traverses. There are both hills and water sceneries in the urban area, which form a unique and beautiful landscape. Lanzhou has been known all around the world as a city of fruits and a summer resort. It is also a famous city of history and culture, scenic resorts include Tulu Valley, Shifo Valley, Wuquan Mountain, and Baita Mountain.

traverse   [trəˈvɜːs]   v. 横贯,穿越

二十八、银川

银川是宁夏回族自治区的省会,位于黄河以西、贺兰山以东,是宁夏政治、经济、文化中心,是发展中的区域性中心城市,中国—阿拉伯国家博览会的永久举办地。银川是历史悠久的古城,是国家历史文化名城,素有"塞上明珠"的美誉。主要名胜古迹有西夏王陵、海宝塔、玉皇阁、南门楼、南关清真寺等。远郊还有风景迷人的苏峪口国家森林公园和引人入胜的镇北堡西部影视城。

Yinchuan

Yinchuan, the capital of Ningxia Hui Autonomous Region, lies to the west of the Yellow River and to the east of Helan Mountain. It is the political, economic and cultural center of the Region as well as a developing regional central city. Yinchuan is the permanent place to hold the Sino-Arabic Expo. It is a national historical and cultural city, known as "the Pearl in the Frontier". The historical sites include the Mausoleum of Xixia Dynasty, Haibao Tower, Yuhuang Pavilion, the South Gate, the Nanguan Mosque, etc. Suburban resorts include the attractive Suyukou National Park and Zhenbeibao Studio City.

frontier ['frʌntɪə] n. 边界,边境

二十九、西安

西安,古称长安,现为陕西省省会,是全省政治、经济、文化、交通的中心。西安地理环境的优越,使它成为中华文明的重要发祥地之一。它还是丝绸之路的起点,拥有七千多年的文明史,三千多年的建城史,一千多年的建都史。在中国历史上,先后有十个朝代建都西安。悠久的历史为西安留下了丰富的文化遗产,西安的文化遗存具有资源密度大、保存好、级别高的特点,游客来到古都西安,到处可寻幽访古,游览观光。秦始皇兵马俑、大雁塔、小雁塔、西安碑林、西安城墙、临潼骊山,都是游客向往的地方。

Xi'an

Xi'an, known as Chang'an in ancient times, is now the capital of Shaanxi Province and its political, economic, cultural and transport center. The benefit of the geographical environment here also made Xi'an a major birthplace of the Chinese civilization. It is also the starting point of the Silk Road. A long history has left behind a rich cultural heritage for Xi'an. Ten dynasties had made it their capitals in Chinese history. The cultural relics in Xi'an are featured in its great density, superb reservation and high level. Visitors to Xi'an, the ancient capital, can enjoy beautiful and scenery sightseeing. Terra-cotta Warriors, Wild Goose Pagoda, Xi'an Forest of Stone Tablets, the Ming Dynasty City Wall, Lishan Mountain in Lintong are the major attractions.

三十、成都

成都是四川省省会,是全省政治、经济、文化中心,位于四川盆地西部,又称"蓉城",拥有三千多年的历史,是国家级历史文化名城。成都是西南地区重要的中心城市,是一个综合性、多功能和对外开放城市。其历史悠久,自然条件得天独厚,灿烂的文化、名胜古迹、民俗风情、古树名花,使它成为一个著名的旅游城市。望江楼、武侯祠、杜甫草堂、都江堰、青城山等都是人们向往的旅游胜地。

Chengdu

Chengdu, the capital and the political, economic, cultural center of Sichuan Province, is located in western Sichuan Basin, with another name as "City of Hibiscus". It has a history of more than 3 000 years, and is a national historical and cultural city. Chengdu is a center city in Southwest China. It is a comprehensive multi-functional and opening-up city. It has become a famous tourism city due to its long history, unique natural conditions, and long-term accumulation to save the splendid culture. There are numerous historical sites, folk customs, and old trees with precious flowers. Major attractions include River-view Pagoda, Memorial Hall of Zhuge Liang, Du Fu's Cottage, Dujiangyan, Mount Qingcheng, and so on.

hibiscus ［hɪˈbɪskəs］ n. 芙蓉,木槿

三十一、重庆

重庆是我国四个直辖市之一,是我国中心城市之一,也是国家历史文化名城,长江上游地区经济中心、金融中心、创新中心,西南地区综合交通枢纽。重庆是一个古老又拥有现代工业的城市,屹立于长江与嘉陵江交汇处,依山就势而建的各种建筑层叠栉比、参差错落、雄伟壮观,人们称它为"山城"。名胜及革命纪念地有北温泉、南温泉、红岩革命纪念馆、缙云山自然保护区等。因重庆每年雾日多达三分之一,又有"雾都"之称。

Chongqing

Chongqing is one of the four municipalities and one of the national central cities. It is also a national historical and cultural city. It is the economic, financial and innovation center of the upper reaches of the Yangtze River region, and the Southwest integrated transport hub. Chongqing is both an ancient and a modern industrial city, standing where the Yangtze River and Jialing River cross. The buildings here are constructed along hillside. That's why Chongqing gets its name as "Mountain City". Major attractions and revolutionary commemoration include the North Hot Springs, South Hot Springs, Hongyan Revolutionary Memorial Hall, Jinyun Mountain Nature Reserve, etc. Chongqing is also called "City of Fog" because foggy days reach up to one third of a year.

integrated ［ˈɪntɪɡreɪtɪd］ adj. 综合的,整合的,完整统一的

三十二、贵阳

贵阳是贵州省省会，位于中国西南云贵高原东部，是我国西南地区重要的中心城市之一，是贵州省的政治、经济、文化、科教、交通中心和西南地区重要的交通通信枢纽。作为喀斯特地貌的典型地区，贵阳拥有以"山奇、水秀、石美、洞异"为特点的喀斯特自然景观和人文旅游资源。既有以山、水、林、洞为特色的高原自然风光，又有文化内涵极为丰富的人文景观。贵阳是中国首批"国家森林城市"之一，被中国气象学会评为"中国避暑之都"。秀丽的风景和良好的气候资源使贵阳被誉为"高原明珠"。

Guiyang

Guiyang, the capital of Guizhou Province, is located in the east of Yunnan-Guizhou Plateau in southwestern China. It is one of the important central cities there. Guiyang is an important transportation and communication hub in southwestern China as well as the political, economic, cultural, scientific, educational, transportation center of Guizhou. The typical karst landscape there brings about unique hills, waters, forests and caves. Guiyang is one of the first "National Forest Cities" in China, and selected as a "Summer City" by the Chinese Meteorological Society. Excellent climate resources, where people feel cool and comfortable especially in the summer, has won Guiyang a reputation of "the Pearl of Plateau".

plateau　［ˈplætəʊ］　n. 高原

meteorological　［ˌmiːtiərəˈlɒdʒɪkl］　adj. 气象的

三十三、昆明

昆明为云南省省会，是国家级历史文化名城，云南省政治、经济、文化、科技、交通中心，是我国重要的旅游、商贸城市。此外，它还是中国面向东南亚、南亚开放的门户枢纽。因夏无酷暑、冬无严寒、气候宜人，具有典型的温带气候特点，年温差为全国城市最小，而有"春城"的美誉。昆明的旅游资源也极为丰富，昆明是全国十大旅游热点城市，首批中国优秀旅游城市，石林、滇池、安宁温泉、九乡、阳宗海等风景名胜都使国内外游客流连忘返。

Kunming

Kunming, capital of Yunnan Province, is a national historical and cultural city. It is the political, economic, cultural, scientific and technological, and transportation center of Yunnan. Kunming is not only an important tourism and trade city of China, but also a gateway hub of China opening up to Southeast Asia and South Asia. Climate here is mild and pleasant with typical temperate climate characteristics. The urban temperature varies very little and thus Kunming is reputed as the "Spring City". The ample tourism resources make Kunming one of the ten tourism cities in China, which include the Stone Forest, Dian Lake, Anning Hot Spring, Jiuxiang, and Yangzong Sea.

三十四、拉萨

拉萨是西藏自治区省会，地处雅鲁藏布江支流拉萨河北岸，海拔约 3 700 米，是世界上海拔最高的城市之一。拉萨是一座具有 1 300 多年历史的古城，是西藏自治区的政治、经济、文化、宗教中心。拉萨全年日照时间在 3 000 小时以上，素有"日光城"的美誉。作为首批中国历史文化名城，拉萨以风光秀丽、历史悠久、民俗风情独特、宗教色彩浓厚而闻名于世，市内的著名景点有布达拉宫、大昭寺、罗布林卡、小昭寺、宗角禄康、河坝林清真寺等。

Lhasa

Lhasa, the capital of Tibet, is located on the northern shore of Lhasa River, a Brahmaputra tributary. With an altitude of 3 700 meters above sea level, it is one of the highest cities in the world. Lhasa is an ancient city with over 1 300 years of history. It is the political, economic, cultural and religious center of Tibet Autonomous Region. Lhasa is renowned as the "Sunshine City" due to its annual sunshine duration of over 3 000 hours. Major attractions of Lhasa include the famous Potala Palace, Jokhang Temple, Norbulingka, Ramoche Temple, Zongjiaolukang, and the Great Mosque, etc.

项目小结

本章节补充了一些航空公司介绍、节日介绍、欢迎词、风景名胜介绍以及各大城市的介绍。通过一系列规范的广播词训练，可以让学生掌握规范的广播词格式，举一反三。

项目训练

1. 在飞往北京的航班上，一些旅客对北京充满向往，假如你是乘务员，应如何用广播介绍北京？

2. 根据旅客兴趣，小组拟写广播词，模仿乘务员和旅客。每个小组在模拟时，其他小组要认真观看，并做好记录。然后根据民航广播播音用语的基本要求进行自我评价，并与其他小组进行互评。

项　　目	考核要点	完成情况	评定等级
客舱广播	播报语气适当		
	广播词格式符合规范		
	广播词地理特色表达准确		
	语音音量适中		
	语调生动		
综合评定等级			

教学支持说明

高等职业学校"十四五"规划民航服务类系列教材系华中科技大学出版社"十四五"期间重点教材。

为了改善教学效果,提高教材的使用效率,满足高校授课教师的教学需求,本套教材备有与纸质教材配套的教学课件(PPT电子教案)和拓展资源(案例库、习题库、视频等)。

为保证本教学课件及相关教学资料仅为教材使用者所用,我们将向使用本套教材的高校授课教师免费赠送教学课件或相关教学资料,烦请授课教师通过电话、邮件或加入旅游专家俱乐部QQ群等方式与我们联系,获取"教学课件资源申请表"文档,准确填写后发给我们,我们的联系方式如下:

地址:湖北省武汉市东湖新技术开发区华工科技园华工园六路

邮编:430223

电话:027-81321911

传真:027-81321917

E-mail:lyzjjlb@163.com

旅游专家俱乐部QQ群号:306110199

旅游专家俱乐部QQ群二维码:

群名称:旅游专家俱乐部
群　号:306110199

教学课件资源申请表

填表时间：_____年___月___日

1. 以下内容请教师按实际情况填写，★为必填项。
2. 学生根据个人情况如实填写，相关内容可以酌情调整提交。

★姓名		★性别	□男 □女	出生年月		★职务	
						★职称	□教授 □副教授 □讲师 □助教

★学校		★院/系	
★教研室		★专业	
★办公电话		家庭电话		★移动电话	
★E-mail（请填写清晰）				★QQ号/微信号	
★联系地址				★邮编	

★现在主授课程情况	学生人数	教材所属出版社	教材满意度
课程一			□满意 □一般 □不满意
课程二			□满意 □一般 □不满意
课程三			□满意 □一般 □不满意
其 他			□满意 □一般 □不满意

教 材 出 版 信 息			
方向一		□准备写 □写作中 □已成稿 □已出版待修订 □有讲义	
方向二		□准备写 □写作中 □已成稿 □已出版待修订 □有讲义	
方向三		□准备写 □写作中 □已成稿 □已出版待修订 □有讲义	

请教师认真填写表格下列内容，提供索取课件配套教材的相关信息，我社将根据每位教师/学生填表信息的完整性、授课情况与索取课件的相关性，以及教材使用的情况赠送教材的配套课件及相关教学资源。

ISBN（书号）	书名	作者	索取课件简要说明	学生人数（如选作教材）
			□教学 □参考	
			□教学 □参考	

★您对与课件配套的纸质教材的意见和建议，希望提供哪些配套教学资源：